1

There is very little in my younger days to indicate that
I would later follow the bent of a bank robber.

—RED RYAN

July 8, 1895

Norman John Ryan is born in a house on Esther Street in the Queen and Spadina neighbourhood of Toronto. His mother, Elizabeth, is attended at the birth by a Dr. Wakeham.

Duck on the rock, hop scotch and nibs formed my early
play days, just the same as that of all my boy friends. I was
nicknamed "Red" and "Chicken" and took part in all of
the games. I used to like to play with the girls, as well as the
boys, and was often called "Sissy" for this. I had great suc-
cess in all of the games I played, and there were none around
our corner who could beat me in a hundred yard race.

—RED RYAN

October 18, 1907

Ryan, aged twelve, is convicted of stealing Dr. Wakeham's bicycle.

> *When I was about twelve years old, one day in the fall of the year, I went with some other boys to an Exhibition. I had 75 cents, I remember, and had spent little of it, when I was attracted by a game which consisted of tossing baseballs into a frame of little square holes, all bearing numbers. We all tried this game as there was a good assortment of prizes which consisted of alarm clocks, jack knives, revolvers, and other articles. I was successful in throwing 4 balls all into number 1 recesses and immediately came into possession of a .22 calibre revolver. Naturally I was the envy of all my boyfriends and was looked upon thereafter as their leader.*
>
> —RED RYAN

1908–1912

Assorted theft and attempted theft convictions, including one for stealing chickens. Also repeated "disorderly conduct" charges. A friend from those days remembered Ryan as "a malicious little bastard." A friend.

> *The following spring I remember mounting a large cherry tree in a neighbour's yard with George. And we were getting our fill of cherries when the lady of the house came out and called to us to come down. "You had better get into the house, old lady," said George, "or*

we will shoot your head off." Quite proud of being so
distinguished, I fired a shot in the air and the rapidity
with which that door was shut just made me swell with
pride. I believe that this was the first actual feeling that
I had of the power of a weapon.

—RED RYAN

December 3, 1912

Ryan makes the front page of the newspapers when he's caught robbing a confectionery. He's convicted on three charges of burglary, theft and shopbreaking, and sentenced to three years in Kingston Penitentiary.

December 13, 1912

The attention Ryan received from the confectionery robbery results in police charging him with an earlier crime, shooting a farmer's horse and blasting a couple of bullets near the farmer's head after the farmer refused to transport Ryan's broken-down, stolen motorcycle into Toronto on his market cart. He's convicted of shooting with intent and sentenced to three-and-a-half years at Kingston Pen, to be served concurrently with the other sentence. When his train pulls out of Toronto for Kingston, he is seen weeping like a child.

In later years, Ryan would blame the encounter with the farmer for his life of crime, saying he was enraged when the farmer ran him down, and fired his shots in anger. In fact, it was an out-of-control Ryan who had rear-ended the farmer's rig. At other times, and in other interviews, Ryan would blame his choice of career on (1) his treatment at

St. John's reformatory, where he was sent at age fourteen, (2) his time in Kingston and (3) his "adventurous disposition" and "vain desire for leadership."

In any event, Ryan's apprentice years were over.

> *Even up to this time I did not know that there was any-thing in my nature except mischieviousness. But events were soon to follow, which marked me in the eyes of my more gentle friends to be shunned and talked about. From these events I was filled with shame and would avoid meet-ing those who I knew talked about me. I think at this time if I had been treated with more generosity I would not have been so sensitive, but who knows.*
>
> —RED RYAN

September 1914–June 1915

As Ryan "wrote" in the *Toronto Star* years later, in one of sev-eral crime-does-not-pay pieces the paper published under his name, when he got out of Kingston after serving twenty-one months of his first stretch, he was "bad." He almost immedi-ately took up armed robbery, first hitting the payroll office of a Toronto piano factory, making off with $1,500, and then robbing the Dominion Express Company "at the point of the revolver," according to the Toronto *Globe*. The take there was a more modest $100. He and his accomplice also stole $2 and a watch from a man on the street.

It's an interesting, if ultimately pointless, exercise to con-sider the question of just when Red Ryan turned "bad." Unlike most of the other famous gangsters of the early decades of the twentieth century, he didn't grow up dirt poor, the bank didn't foreclose on the farm, his father didn't abandon the family when Ryan was a boy and he didn't have to steal to support his mother and siblings. By all accounts, the Ryan family was a respectable, working-class bunch. His parents both came from Irish stock. Red's father was a sheet-metal worker, and Red was the fourth of seven children. He was a red-haired, blue-eyed charmer with a record that stretched back to his pre-teens.

Red's brother Frank apparently made some money running booze across the U.S. border during prohibition, but other than that, no family members had any trouble with the law. Ryan's biographer Peter McSherry claims Ryan's father, John, was a violent man who favoured older son Frank and regularly tried to slap younger son Norman into shape, but he wasn't the only disobedient boy being slapped around by a parent back in those days. If Red was jealous of the attention aimed at his brother, and if engaging in violent crime was the best he could come up with as a way to turn some of that spotlight on himself, maybe he was just naturally bad. Certainly there is no moment in his life, at least no moment that I've been able to discover, when, confronted by a choice, Ryan made the right one. So if not born bad, I think it's safe to say he was born with a severely limited imagination.

There's another aspect of the Ryan family story that differs from the standard gangster narrative, in which the wayward son, no matter how many banks he robs or cops he shoots, is always loved, sheltered and alibi-ed: Ryan's family was ashamed of him. Early in Red's career, his younger brother

Russ changed his last name to Walsh, in an attempt to escape the taint associated with Ryan. One of his younger sisters tried to alert the authorities about what Red was up to, near the end. Ryan would have been well aware of his family's feelings towards him, but if he was capable of an honest assessment of his life, he would have also been well aware that he had earned every bit of it.

Ryan himself—and I can't stress enough that he should never be believed about any aspect of his life—was perhaps approaching honesty when he wrote this about his family: "I had an exceptionally good father and mother, and all of the members of my family were held in high regard, and always have been, regardless of the loss of pride which came through my escapades." But that was written shortly before a court date, so the building up of his family in order to give more weight to his own self-deprecation has to be viewed as tactics, as much as anything else.

The truth is usually the simplest explanation. The Ryans were a normal family with a bad kid who, whether due to a lack of parental affection as a child or not, could never get enough of the attention he craved.

Planning to make his way west after the two armed robberies, Ryan made it as far as Owen Sound, Ontario, where, according to the *Globe*, he was arrested "after an all-day chase through the woods and a revolver fight with constables and a posse." It ended with Ryan and his partner caught trying to paddle their way to freedom in a leaking rowboat. "The arrests nipped in the bud what promised to be a career of serious crime," the *Globe* reported.

Name	Norman J. Ryan	Distinctive marks-etc
Alias		
Age	19	Scar R. eyebrow
Where born	Toronto	
Height	5.10½	Grey spot R. eyebrow
Weight	145	
Complexion	Fair	
Eyes	Blue	
Hair	Red	
Occupation	Cook	
Sentence	8 years	
Date of	June 16 - 1915	
Where Sentenced	Owen Sound	
Crime	Burglary	
Remarks		
	Industrial School (2)	
	die 4578	

Name	John W. Turner	Distinctive marks-etc
Alias		
Age	22	Scar back R. middle finger
Where born	Toronto	
Height	5.7¾	between 1st and 2nd join
Weight	150	
Complexion	Dark	Scar back knuckle 12 year
Eyes	Blue	R. forefinger
Hair	D. Brown	
Occupation	Labourer	
Sentence	2 years	
Date of	June 16 - 1915	
Where Sentenced	Owen Sound	
Crime	Burglary	
Remarks		

Name	John Wilson	Distinctive marks-etc
Alias		
Age	26	Crossed eyes
Where born	Belleville Ont.	
Height	5.5	Nose crooked (been broken)
Weight	128	
Complexion	Medium	
Eyes	Grey	
Hair	Brown	
Occupation	Liveryman	
Sentence	4 years	
Date of	June 16 - 1915	
Where Sentenced	Belleville with	
	House Breaking intent	
Remarks		

Name	Oscar Williams	Distinctive marks-etc
Alias		
Age	27	R. ring finger deformed
Where born	Ottawa	
Height	5.7½	Scar outside R. hand
Weight	155	
Complexion	Fair	Brown mark L. side bridge
Eyes	Brown	of nose
Hair	L. Brown	
Occupation	Waiter	Ruptured
Sentence	3 years	
Date of	June 17 - 1915	
Where Sentenced	Ottawa	
Crime	Theft from the person	
Remarks	with violence	
	See 396 also	
	Stewart the thief	

Ryan was sent back to Kingston for eight years by a judge in Owen Sound for burglary (a stolen motorcycle) and shooting at the police "with intent to maim." The following November, he was brought from Kingston to Toronto, where he was sentenced to twelve years for the two armed robberies. He had just turned twenty years old, and you could be forgiven for believing that the *Globe* was right, and Ryan would slowly moulder away, forgotten, behind the walls at Kingston.

But Red Ryan hadn't even started.

March 26, 1918

Frank Rasky included a chapter on Ryan in a Harlequin paperback he wrote in 1958 called *Gay Canadian Rogues*, a title that offers writers and publishers a cautionary lesson about something, although I'm not quite sure what. Rasky writes that prison officials called Ryan "the weeper" and that "soft-hearted officials *always* paroled him. He was such a clean-cut, six-foot-tall fellow, with wide, blue eyes."

But weeping wasn't required to get out of jail in 1918. Men were needed to fight the Great War, and Red Ryan decided to join the army. He signed up on March 26 and, after some papers were stamped, walked out the door with a full pardon in his hands. Of course, he had to go to England and join his battalion, but he made sure he never had to fight.

A Crown attorney, arguing a case against Ryan years later, had this to say in court about his military career: "He got as far as England, and I am sorry to say his military record was no better than his record in civil life." According to long-time *Toronto Star* reporter, and Ryan's chief ghostwriter, Roy

Greenaway, the only logical interpretation of Ryan's military record is that he was a coward and a deserter. "He was always in trouble when there was any chance to go to the front."

He hadn't been in England long when he got drunk, got in a fight and stole some chickens (again!). A disciplinary infraction resulted in Ryan being confined to barracks, so he went AWOL. The civilian authorities in London arrested him for robbing a grocery store. After serving his sentence, he was handed back to the military, court-martialled and locked up in the camp guardhouse, from which he escaped through a skylight.

Now he was officially a deserter, but hey, at least the war was over. It was November 1918.

1919–1920

According to Peter McSherry, the next two years of Ryan's life are a "dark chapter" about which very little is known.

But I can fairly confidently assert the following: He either did or didn't join the Foreign Legion in Africa. He either did or didn't join the English Merchant Navy. He either did or didn't assault an Australian soldier, steal his identity papers and make his way to Australia. The Australian soldier either was or wasn't actually an Australian seaman, who was thrown overboard by Ryan after he stole the papers. He either did or didn't rob banks in England, Ireland and Australia.

Eventually, he came back to Toronto.

Well, I soldiered, though I had my trouble in the army, and after I sailed around for a time I came back to Canada, and

right there is where I should have made good. My reputa-
tion, however, always followed me, and it was not long before
I found solace in the old environments and the craving for
excitement got the best of me.

—RED RYAN

September 1920–September 1922

"The Lone Bandit" began hitting banks in Hamilton, Ontario, in the summer of 1921. Shortly after that, he expanded his operations to include Montreal. He was daring and reckless. Bullets flew. He had style. Counters were vaulted. The newspapers loved him. They came up with the nickname.

Of course, none of this could possibly have anything to do with our man, who, after returning home from his overseas adventures in September 1920, was living a respectable life in Toronto, east of Hamilton and west of Montreal.

His father had died while he was away, and his mother died shortly after his return. Ryan was working as a tinsmith and supporting his three young sisters. And he was engaged to be married, to a young woman from Heart's Content in Newfoundland. They were hitched in late August 1921 and travelled to Winnipeg for their honeymoon.

While she was still in Winnipeg, Ryan having left her with an

RED RYAN'S NICKNAMES

- The Golden Boy of Crime
- Kingston's Public Exhibit No. 1
- The Ace of Canadian Bank Robbers
- The Lone Bandit
- The Big Red Fox
- Ontario's pet boy
- Ontario's prodigal boy
- Canada's Jesse James

excuse, Elsie Ryan (née Sharpe) apparently received word that her new husband was in jail. He was the Lone Bandit. According to McSherry, Elsie fainted on the spot.

Ryan's arrest happened in Montreal on October 26, 1921, after what the *Globe* described as "a vicious gun battle with detectives."

13

In Ryan's telling, he and his accomplice/getaway driver George McVittie thought they were holed up in "the safest possible spot at the Young Men's Christian Association," when they were "surrounded and bowled over." As soon as they realized the police were outside the building, the men decided to make a run for it, so Red gave McVittie a gun and grabbed another for himself. When they exited the YMCA building, again according to Ryan, "Bullets were flying in all directions." So Red went back in for more guns. "We were both well heeled then," he wrote later.

The two men ran out, Red leading, firing shots in all directions. Ryan saw at least five police detectives, who were all shooting back. McVittie made for the street, attempting to get to their car, despite Red telling him to stick close to the wall of the building, and the two robbers were separated. Ryan kept to the wall, dodging bullets and firing back at the police, "emptying my second gun high and low." As he was reloading, one of the detectives sneaked up behind him, grabbed him and threw him to the ground. They began wrestling.

> *At first the detective got both arms around my chest and I rolled over and all but got the upper hand. He caught me by the throat and I struggled frantically to get a half Nelson and roll him over. His hold was firm, however, and I couldn't budge, doubled up as I was.*
> *The rest came up and it was all over.*
> —RED RYAN

On November 1, 1921, Ryan and McVittie were sentenced to seven years and fourteen lashes for two counts of armed robbery with violence in Montreal. Eleven months later they were back in court in Hamilton to face similar charges. McVittie was found guilty of robbing one bank with Ryan and was sentenced to ten years. Ryan—the "arch criminal," according to McVittie's lawyer—was convicted of robbing two banks, attempting to rob a third and shooting at a bank teller. He was sentenced to twenty-five years in Kingston. As he left the courtroom, he was overheard joking with a sheriff's officer that the judge "was mighty free with another man's time." His days of crying like a child after sentencing were well behind him.

One other item from the coverage of Ryan's arrest is worth noting. A story in the *Globe* out of London, Ontario, said that police there believed Ryan was the wanted "fourth man" who had evaded capture after a man was murdered during a bank robbery in the nearby small town of Melbourne. They felt certain Ryan was the wanted killer because of the gun he was carrying when he was arrested. If the London police were correct, this would have been the first time Ryan was placed at the scene of a murder.

Red Ryan was heading back to Kingston Penitentiary, and with no world war to bail him out, it looked as if he'd be gone a good long while.

It ended up being less than a year.

FIVE FUGITIVES LANDED FINALLY IN LAW'S NET

Long Arm of the Law Finally Gathers in Last of Gang

FOUR OF THE QUINTET ARE TAKEN ALIVE

TO GET GLASS OF BEER BUYS TWO GLASSES

Lest We Forget

Do You Remember When?

NEW MEMBERS OF SENATE ANNOUNCED AT VARSITY

Packers and Shippers

HILL, the MOVER

Wash Away That Itch!

D.D.D.

FREE

CHAPTER 2

ALMOST EVERYTHING

2

One day, I received an email from an editor at a big publishing house, asking me if I had ever considered writing a book. He wrote that he liked my work and would be interested in talking to me about an idea he had that he thought would suit me. We set up a time to talk on the phone.

"Have you ever heard of Red Ryan?" he asked me. "He was a bank robber." The name rang a faint bell, and the editor started filling me in on some of the basic facts of Ryan's life. Suddenly, the bell rang clearly.

"Hang on," I said. "I know who this guy is. Morley Callaghan wrote a novel about him. I read it a long time ago."

The sound of googling came down the line.

"Holy shit!" he said. "You're right." My sense was that he took it as a sign. I know I did.

For a large chunk of my younger life, if you had asked me to name my favourite author, I would have said Callaghan. His deceptively simple, clear style appealed to me, but there was more than that. There was a purity in Callaghan's writing. You always sensed a questing, by both the author and his characters, to realize their best selves. I felt there was something profoundly good about him.

So the idea of developing a project that might include Callaghan, even briefly, had some appeal. But I still wasn't sure I wanted to write a book about a bank robber.

The man from the publishing house said he'd send me some newspaper clippings on Ryan, and we left it at that.

I should point out here that while this was going on I was wrestling with a journalism project of my own. Would you understand what I meant if I said I was trying to create a small space in the mainstream media for an objective assessment of events and opinion?

We used to claim that journalism by its nature was unbiased and objective, but that was a long time ago. Or, at least, it feels like a long time ago. Back in the 1980s, my first newspaper editor told me that if all the liberals thought I was a conservative, and all the conservatives thought I was a liberal, that meant I was doing my job. But the days when it was possible to achieve that kind of perfect journalistic equilibrium seemed to be long gone, and in a small way, I was trying to bring them back on the radio.

It was my naive belief that it was still possible to open up little windows of communication between the political silos by challenging conventional wisdom and exposing our listeners to a broader range of opinion. At a time when the reinforcement of previously held points of view seemed to be journalism's primary function, my team and I were trying to reintroduce the concept of surprise.

Our radio program was built to question orthodoxies, which is always a challenge. But I was facing another challenge: the question of style. Put simply, I believe a current affairs interview show is about the guests, not the host. When I hear a host start talking about himself, or herself, I reach for the off button. That's one thing.

Also, an emotional exploration of issues doesn't interest me. An intellectual exploration does. I don't want to hear a personal story unless it can be expanded to make a larger, intellectual point. And even then, keep it short and don't milk the hell out of it. Sadly for me, this is the age of the personal story.

The best description I've read of my approach to journalism was in a book about something else entirely: *Zen and the Art of Motorcycle Maintenance,* by Robert Pirsig. Pirsig wrote that there are two ways of viewing the world, two modes employed to try to come to an understanding of things: the classic mode and the romantic mode. The classic mode, he said, is straightforward, unadorned and economical: "Its purpose is not to inspire emotionally, but to bring order out of chaos and make the unknown known." The romantic mode, on the other hand, is more inspirational and imaginative: "Feelings rather than facts predominate."

A romantic sees the classic approach as dull, while an

employer of the classic style sees the romantic as frivolous and shallow. Without substance. As this is a particularly romantic age of journalism, I was feeling more and more like a visitor from another time.

So, this is what was going on when a large box of newspaper clippings arrived, chronicling the rise and fall, and rise and fall, and rise and fall of an overrated bank robber named Norman Ryan.

Right off the bat it was clear that the journalism was awful. Names and dates were all over the place. The *Star*'s court reporting didn't match the *Globe*'s court reporting. Stories appeared for no reason other than to tell the reader not to believe other stories. It was a mess. But a wild, fascinating mess. And, at least when it came to the day-to-day beat reporting, it was an understandable mess. Reporters were relying on their notes, their memories and the very few official documents that were available. And those official documents were also, often, a product of half-assed note taking and faulty memory.

The feature articles were another thing altogether. The default mode for the feature writer in the fedora era was a seen-it-all world-weariness. Nobody was putting anything over on these guys. And yet they were conned, spun and deked until they were dizzy. Most of their stories were complete works of fiction, pure propaganda, and it was clear that these hard-boiled newsmen didn't have a clue that what they were doing wasn't journalism, in any real sense of the word; it was public relations, ego building for the various romantics whose causes they were supplying with oxygen. After it all went south and the real Ryan was revealed, most of them wrote look-back pieces in which everyone else was fooled, but not them. Ryan never seemed right to them, they would claim. He always smelled fishy. And why not write that? Why not try to make themselves look good after the fact? Reputation and self-regard were all that mattered to them. They were romantics too. Besides, who was going to check?

It was an unholy construction of slippery, dubious facts, with myth used as mortar to fill in the gaps. Some of it cost people their lives. And standing in the centre, basking in it all, was the spiritual grandfather of all the Trumps, Hiltons and Kardashians that followed, the pure, uncut, spotlight-craving romantic—Red Ryan.

Another thing I discovered was that this story didn't feature just Ryan and Callaghan. Hemingway was there, for God's sake. And the prime minister of Canada.

Journalism, literature and politics. The story had it all. And the fact that almost all this tawdry business took place in the uptight, sanctimonious Protestant backwater of Toronto (my hometown) gave the whole thing an underpinning of irony that I liked very much too.

I told the editor I was in. I actually did want to write a book about a bank robber. My last piece of long-form journalism had been a documentary about Nothing. In this story, I saw the potential to write about almost everything. I could probably even find a way to squeeze in *Zen and the Art of Motorcycle Maintenance*.

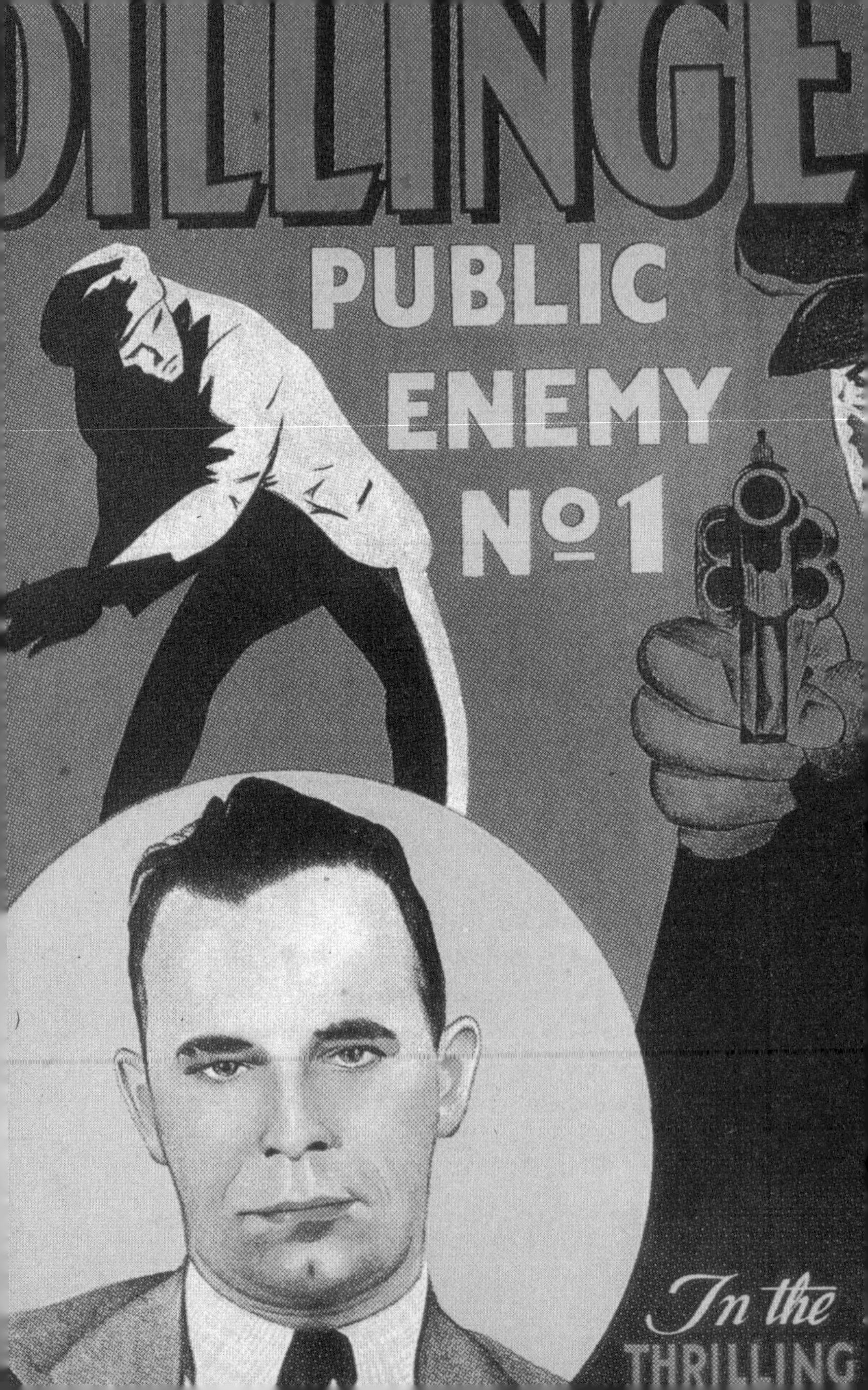
DILLINGE
PUBLIC
ENEMY
No 1
In the
THRILLING

CHAPTER 3

THE UNDEAD

3

Just to be clear, Red Ryan is dead. He always has been. At least, he has been ever since he was shot and killed in 1936. I think it's important to point this out because you would be surprised by the number of outlaws—some of them quite famous—who didn't die when they were supposed to. John Dillinger, for one. He's probably still kicking around somewhere. A hundred and sixteen years old and feisty as all hell. I mean, why not? Jesse James lived to the ripe old age of 103.

That last statement probably requires some explanation, particularly if you've been living under the mistaken notion that Jesse James was shot in the back by the Coward Robert Ford back in 1882.

Over the decades following the shooting, countless men came forward claiming to be Jesse James, but all their stories were shot full of holes—all of them, except for J. Frank Dalton.

Dalton first popped up in the late 1940s, round about the hundredth anniversary of James's birth. That was no accident. He told the press that Ford had actually shot another member of the James gang, a man named Bigelow, whose face and head had been shot up so bad that it gave him, Jesse, an idea. He had wanted to leave the outlaw life anyway, so he decided to pretend the body was his. He claimed that the governor of Missouri at the time had been in on the misdirection play. All the gang members made a pledge to each other not to betray the secret until they each reached one hundred years of age, and since Dalton/James claimed he'd just turned a hundred, he was now telling his story.

Nothing the old man said could be disproved. Even his scars were in all the right places.

Dalton was set up as the feature attraction at a roadside tourist stop along Route 66, where he would happily entertain visitors with his stories of the James gang. Unless those visitors were journalists, that is. Apparently, he grew to hate reporters so much, he took to pulling out his six-shooter and firing at the ceiling of his cabin to scare them away. I recommend this technique, by the way. Reporters can be awfully tough to get rid of, once they've locked on to your scent, and they are generally scared of loud noises.

J. Frank Dalton, a.k.a. Jesse James, finally died in August

1951. If he really was who he claimed to be, he would have been just three weeks short of his 104th birthday.

Butch Cassidy was another unkillable outlaw. You probably believe that he and the Sundance Kid were shot to death by the Bolivian army in 1908. No, he lived out his life as a machinist in Spokane, Washington. He called himself William T. Phillips, and didn't actually die until 1937, after a long life spent leaving little clues around about his real identity for wild west "historians" to uncover later.

Even John "Red" Hamilton, the pride of Sault Ste. Marie, Ontario, who ran with John Dillinger and is best known, according to his Wikipedia page, "for his lingering death and secret burial," was still around more than ten years after that death, according to his nephew Bruce, who met him on a family trip to the Soo in 1946. Now that's what I call lingering.

According to the official version of events, Red Hamilton, whose other nickname, the result of a toboggan accident as a child, was Three-Finger Jack, was shot in the back by a police deputy with a rifle outside St. Paul, Minnesota, in late April 1934, as he, Dillinger and another gang member named Homer Van Meter were attempting to elude the cops in a stolen vehicle. Red was sitting in the back seat of the car. The bullet that hit him had passed through the car body and the seat cushion, and the force of the blast had thrown him against the back of the front seat.

After about a fifty-mile-long chase, with both sides firing at each other the entire way, the gang members finally shook off the police. Hamilton was losing blood quickly, so Dillinger decided to take him to Chicago for treatment. The gang stole another car, ditched the bloody one they had been using, and off they flew.

By the time they reached Chicago, Hamilton's wound was festering. Gangrene was setting in and he was in terrible shape. Dillinger couldn't find a doctor to treat his partner, probably because they were all scared about what would happen if one of Dillinger's friends died under their care, so he took Red to a gang hideout in a local tavern to die. After three days there, he was starting to smell very bad from the gangrene, but he still wasn't dying, so Red was moved to a safe house that was being rented by a gang member and his girlfriend. The girlfriend tended to Hamilton until, finally, he died, almost a week after being shot.

The official version goes on to say that Dillinger and Van Meter buried their friend near Oswego, Illinois, after liberally covering him with watered-down lye to make it harder to identify the remains.

That's the official version. Nephew Bruce's version is a little different.

He says his father, Wilton, and his uncle Foye, Red's brothers, both received large sums of money in the mid-1940s that had been hidden away by the Dillinger gang, money that only a living member of that gang would have been able to find. Bruce's father used his to buy a new house and a car. Uncle Foye bought a machine shop in Rockford, Illinois, and an island in the Great Lakes, somewhere near Sault Ste. Marie, along with assorted boats and a seaplane. It was in a large cabin on this island, Bruce says, that his uncle Red lived.

Apparently, he'd been able to get his wound treated after

all. After a period of convalescence with another brother in Indiana, Red had recovered enough to work for a couple of years in a bowling alley before heading back to Canada. According to one of Red's sisters, he died in the 1970s.

So that's the alternate history of Red Hamilton. Would you like to hear what really happened to Dillinger?

Obviously someone was shot by the G-men outside the Biograph Theater in Chicago on July 22, 1934, after watching *Manhattan Melodrama*, starring Clark Gable and Myrna Loy. Someone was walking out of the movie house with Dillinger's girlfriend Polly Hamilton (no relation to Red) and Anna Sage, the notorious Woman in Red. But was that someone John Dillinger, Public Enemy No. 1? Or was it some guy named Jimmie Lawrence, a small-time crook with a terminal disease who agreed, for a large chunk of money, to take Dillinger's

THE GOLDEN BOY OF CRIME

place? Did Dillinger pay the FBI agent who fired the fatal shots ten grand to shoot the wrong man and then switch a card with Dillinger's real fingerprints on it for the card of the prints taken from the dead man?

But what about the corpse's resemblance to the real Dillinger, you ask? Well, there may have been some plastic surgery involved there. I'm not saying there was. I'm not saying there wasn't.

All I know is you don't have to spend too much time poking around online before you find people convinced that John Dillinger lived out the rest of his life in Oregon, happily married to a Native American woman . . . or that he worked as a machinist (just like Butch and Uncle Foye) in California, where one of his "biographers" may have actually interviewed him in a darkened room, over thirty years after his death.

Now, you can dismiss all this if you want. You can write it off as the work of internet crackpots who really should find a more productive outlet for their energies, but I can tell you with a great deal of confidence that these truth seekers put considerably more effort and research into their work than the press covering Red Ryan did. And if every single "fact" they've uncovered and every buried secret they've unearthed is completely, unquestionably, 100 percent bogus, that just means that their record of accuracy is pretty much the same as that of the press covering Red Ryan.

Either way, I like to picture old John Dillinger, sometime in the 1960s perhaps, taking a long road trip up to Canada and visiting Red Hamilton on his island. Doing a little swimming. Maybe going out to catch some pike.

Now, OUTLAW BUFFS will tell you that when it came to being a crook, John Dillinger was playing in a higher league than our man, Red Ryan. But if you think he wasn't capable of messing up a robbery once in a while, let me tell you what happened one spring afternoon in 1934, when the Dillinger gang tried to make an extrajudicial withdrawal from a bank in Mason City, Iowa.

This should have been a very successful heist. The bank had close to a quarter of a million dollars on hand, and the robbers were basically an all-star team. Besides their leader, John Dillinger, and Three-Finger Jack Hamilton, the gang included Eddie Green, who also worked with Ma Barker. He was considered an expert "jug marker," which is what the old-time crooks called the men who staked out the banks beforehand and planned the getaway routes. Homer Van Meter was also in the crew. He was Dillinger's associate for almost ten years, and was known as the prankster of the bunch. The wheelman was another long-time Dillinger gang member, a former boxer named Tommy Carroll. And also along for the job, stationed outside with his eye on the doors, was the noted psychopath and automatic weapons aficionado Baby Face Nelson, who was responsible for killing more FBI agents than anyone who ever lived.

But despite that lineup, the robbery was a fiasco.

When the bank president noticed Van Meter walking in the door with his machine gun, he ran into his office with the keys to the vault and bolted the door. Homer took a few shots at the door, but decided to help empty out the tellers' cash drawers instead of pursuing the matter further.

Alerted by the racket Van Meter was making, one of the tellers barricaded himself in the room with the vault, locking the door behind him. That's where Red Hamilton found him. But the door to that room couldn't be opened either. Red saw the teller, and the stacks of money on the shelves around him, by looking through a slot in the door. So Red poked his gun in the door slot and ordered the teller to start passing him the stacks of bills through the slot, which the teller did, slowly. Eventually Red noticed that the teller was passing him only the stacks of one-dollar bills. He could see the higher-denomination bills piled everywhere, but the teller wouldn't pass him any of those, no matter how much Red threatened him. Red couldn't shoot him, of course, because then he'd get nothing, so he was forced to watch in frustration as the very cool teller kept slowly passing him the ones. (I should point out here that some accounts of the robbery describe the door the teller shut behind him as being barred, like the door of a jail cell. But I prefer the image of the slot.)

Out in the main room of the bank, Eddie Green was hit in the back by a tear gas canister that had been fired by a guard in an elevated bulletproof observation booth. Green fired a couple of shots in retaliation, shattering the "bulletproof" glass, but missing the guard.

Meanwhile, a police officer who happened to look out

a window in a building across the street saw what was happening and took a shot at Dillinger, who was on the sidewalk guarding prisoners, hitting him in the arm. Dillinger turned and fired a blast from his machine gun at the window, forcing the cop to duck out of the way. Dillinger decided then that it was time to go.

Van Meter was sent to fetch Red Hamilton, who was still slowly collecting one-dollar bills through his door slot. He later said he figured there was two hundred grand still sitting in the room with the teller when he left. He also said he wished he'd shot the man.

When Hamilton ran out of the bank, the same cop that had shot Dillinger popped back up in his window and took a shot at Red, hitting him in the shoulder.

All the crooks piled into the getaway car after forcing twenty hostages to stand on the car's running boards and bumpers, completely surrounding it with a human shield. Then they drove, very slowly because of all the people weighing down the car, out of town, with the police, very slowly, following them. A few miles out of town, Baby Face Nelson got out of the car and started blasting at the pursuers with his machine gun until, eventually, the police turned back. Then the hostages were released and the gang sped away.

Out of the quarter of a million dollars in the bank in Mason City, the Dillinger gang withdrew a little over fifty thousand.

By the way, every single man who took part in that robbery was shot to death, either by the police, the FBI or both, within a year. Except for the ones who weren't.

THE TORONTO DAILY STA

...EAR. THIRTY PAGES. TORONTO, TUESDAY, SEPTEMBER 11, 1923. 5 O'CLOCK

...CAPED KINGSTON CONVICTS STILL A...

...ICTS BREAK AWAY ...ROM SWAMP REFUGE

...nsford and Guards ...rsuing Them in ...otor Cars

...LOODHOUNDS

...at Large—Convict ...to Prevent Escape

...Star by a Staff Reporter. ...Mills, Sept. 11.—The ...ve escaped north- ...McAdoo's Woods and ...nsford is pursuing ...in motor cars. It is ...convicts are heing ...Lake on the north- ...gston Mills.

...Star by a Staff Reporter. ...ept. 11.—With four of ...ts who made a sensa- ...from the penitentiary ...at large this morning ...are being made to ...ounds to assist in the ...was also received this ...W. S. Hughson, in- ...ntentiaries, that a re- ...will be paid for the ...h of the escaped con-

...n still at large, and ...ed to be hiding in the ...mp between the Perth ...Cataraqui river to- ...n Mills, are:

...son, Toronto, serving ...robbery.

...wn, Toronto, serving ...highway robbery.

...n, alias Norman Slade, ...enced to 25 years and ...k robbery.

...ans, Montreal, serving ...manslaughter.

...Mullen, serving four ...r robbing a bank at ...ario, also escaped, but ...d three miles from the ...with the loss of blood ...ot wound in the hand, ...a guard who fired on ...hey escaped.

...Out All Night

...g the guards had been ... They were cold and ...ners were driving in to ...working in the fields. ...o posses. Everyone in ...e seemed content to ...of man-hunting to the ...man-hunters. The ...etely surrounded the ...and were especially ...e east side to prevent ...from breaking across ...l and getting into the ...he Rideau river. From ...ight make their way ...ible to get food at the ... Everyone was cold ...t there was news.

...bout eleven o'clock on ...uddy road overgrown ...h that divides the ...acres of bush into a ...th half, four guards ...n horseback were sta- ...s so dark the scout ...his horse's head. But ...fence wires on the ...the road creek. He ...e guards who were ...he road and then there ...The four men had their

...dark there was a rush ...d. The guards fired ...at the sound and rush- ...in the dark a man's ...Are you hurt, shorty?" ...shot again where the ...rom and one of them ...ank as a man tashed ...l the north side of the ...n had crossed from the ...f the woods to the ...of the seven hundred ...fifteen rifle shots were ...ark. No one knows if ...hit. There is no blood ...no bodies.

...Heavy Wrench

...n came up this morn- ...found a hammer and ...ch that the men had ...n they were fired on ...the road. These were ...ompson's car and had ...s weapons when they ...woods. A few yards ...road was a prisoner's ...se gray-blue Sherlock ...d caps that all the ...r.

...the ground where the ...red with Warden Pons- ...ning. He had nothing ...blication but is confi- ...the men crossed into ...tract during the night, ...guards say they think ...ly three.

...sford would not say ...attery of R. C. H. A. ...would be called out to ...rdon around the woods ...y prison guards, who ...men by sight and are ...ed in this sort of work. ...ightening ring and beat ...r the convicts. There ...vance, probably of this ...e to-day.

...of Man Seen

...e o'clock word was ...warden by one of the ...ng the northern fron- ...oods that traces of one ...n found where he had ...a fence along the road ...he woods on the north. ...an unconfirmed report ...had seen one or two ...the road early this ...the men escape out of ...l of the woods it will ...se. There are several

GORDON SIMPSON

one of the convicts who escaped from Kingston penitentiary yesterday. He was serving a ten-year term following his conviction in Hamilton, Toronto and Guelph for a series of robberies.

MOTHER, ON WAY TO HER SICK BABY, HAS DISAPPEARED

Police are Searching for Mrs. Frank Vanone, Attractive 19-Year-Old Mother

ON WAY TO THE FALLS

Police have been asked to assist in the search for Mrs. Frank Vanone, attractive 19-year-old mother of Lindsay, who has disappeared.

On Friday, August 17, Mrs. Vanone, who was with her husband, a member of the Maple Leaf vaudeville company, left by C.P.R. train for her home in Niagara Falls, N.Y., in response to a message from her mother that her baby was seriously ill. Hearing nothing from her, either as to her arrival or the condition of the child, Mr. Vanone became anxious, and on instituting enquiry found that his wife had not reached her home, and, although diligent search has been made, nothing has been heard of her. Mrs. Vanone was an attractive looking girl, 19 years old, fair complexion, with bobbed hair. When she left Lindsay she was wearing a heavily figured sand-colored crepe de chine dress, black cape with grey lamb collar and fringe at the bottom, blue sandals and black stockings. The Toronto police have been notified and ask that information concerning her be forwarded to them.

REPAIR WIRES TO TOKIO

Now in Telegraphic Communication With Outside World

Special to Star Weekly by United Press.

San Francisco, Cal., Sept. 11.—Direct radio and land wire communication was established with Tokio to-day for the first time since the earthquake. Telegraph wires were restored between Tokio and the Iwaki radio station at Tomioka, Japan, a distance of 144 miles. Iwaki radio is in direct communication with the radio corporation station here.

CLOSE BATHING AREAS

The protected bathing areas at Fisherman's Island, Olympic Island and Bathurst street were closed to-day for the season by the life savers and the public are warned not to bathe in these areas again this season. Sunnyside and Scarboro Beach areas are still open for bathing.

EXPECT GERMAN CAVE-IN

Paris, Sept. 11. — Capitulation by Germany is regarded in France as imminent. One journal, L'Intransigeant, usually regarded as conservative, goes so far as to predict it will occur within a few days, if not within a few hours.

MME. PONAFIDINE FLED ACROSS ICE TO ESCAPE SOVIET

Now in Toronto, She Tells of Sufferings She Underwent

TRAGEDY OF RUSSIA

Tried Thorough Communism, and All Industry Stopped Dead--Some Better Now

A grey-eyed, grey-haired woman, with a manner of gentle gravity and charm, a woman whose life has been lived in all the places of the world's romance and tragedy, is Madame Pierre Ponafidine, the guest of Lady Poynter, in Toronto this week.

Born of American parents in Persia, Madame Ponafidine married a Russian diplomat, with whom she lived for many years in various countries in Asia and Europe. They settled finally on her husband's estate between Petrograd and Moscow in 1903, and lived there among the peasants until the war, and later the Russian revolution made chaos and disaster of the life of the Russian nobility.

One of the Old Order

In her eyes, when she speaks, there is the reflection of the tragedy of that unhappy country. Madame Ponafidine belongs to the old order of Russia, an order in which the rapid and confusing movement of history has been thrust further and further into the past. Two events, which she related to The Star, spelt the history, not only of her own family, but of the whole society of Russia. When her brother-in-law died, the late emperor of Russia was among the pall-bearers at the funeral. When her sister-in-law died, after Russia had fallen into anarchy and confusion, her daughters dragged her body on a sledge outside the city and buried it with their own hands.

But it is not as a member of the old order that Madame Ponafidine takes her stand against the Russia of to-day.

"If I thought that the ruin of my husband, the scattering of my loved ones meant the bettering of one life—one single life—in Russia, I would say: 'They were perhaps right. We deserved it,'" she said, "but this is not the case. Russia to-day, has lost all its culture, all its education, all its fear of God. It is fighting everything that we know to be holy and high. It has abolished the authority of the school, the home and the government. It claims that it is impossible to hold at the same time the tenets of socialism and religion."

Fled Across Volga

From the time the revolution broke out until a year and a half ago, when, through the assistance of American friends, she finally made her escape from Russia, Madame Ponafidine lived constantly under the surveillance of the soviet government. That escape itself was one of those extraordinary adventures that have no parallel in any history except that of the last half dozen years. She fled with her son and a group of friends across the Volga, stepping from one cake of ice to another under the blinding glare of the searchlights of the bolsheviks.

"My friends and family in Russia?" she said. "Some of them are dead, some of them exiled, many of them lost. For many months I did not dare to make any but the vaguest references to my own escape for fear it might jeopardize the chances of those who were left behind."

For three years she was literally

(Continued on Page Two)

PICKED UP UNCONSCIOUS; WATCH AND MONEY GONE

Special to The Star by United Press.

Erie, Pa., Sept. 11.—Charles Lewis, of Toronto, was picked up in an unconscious condition by a passerby on a main road near this city late last night suffering from injuries which he was unable to account for. He declared he had a large amount of money and a gold watch, which were missing when he was picked up.

NEAR FIVE-MILLION MARK.

Washington, Sept. 11. — Early returns from Red Cross chapters throughout the country to-day showed total contributions to Japan relief of $4,834,000, and forecast passing of the $5,000,000 minimum during the day.

Favorable Report by Dr. H. B. Jeffs' Made on New Tuberculosis Serum

That Dr. H. B. Jeffs, M.B., graduate of the University of Toronto in 1914, and now Canadian immigration advisor in London, recently made a report on the subject of the Spahlinger serum for treatment of tuberculosis, was the statement made to-day to The Star by Dr. Jeffs' father, Dr. W. H. Jeffs, of Yonge street.

"My son made a report on the subject for the Canadian government some time ago," said the father of Dr. Jeffs to-day, "and I understand it was favorable, but beyond this fact ... well of the discovery."

The weight of opinion as expressed by several medical men of Toronto to whom The Star spoke to-day with regard to the Spahlinger serum, was to the effect that this reported discovery of some months ago, is still in the experimental stages.

Dr. W. J. Dobbie, medical superintendent of the Weston Sanatorium, and who is actively associated with the work carried on by the Gage Institute in this city, said he knew nothing about the serum beyond what he had read from time to time. "As far as I know it has not been

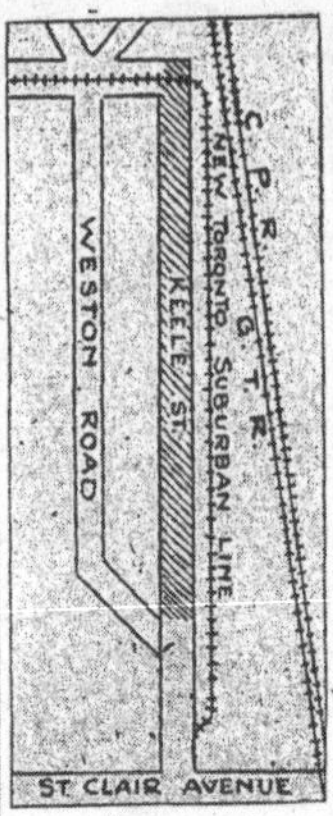

CLOSE THIS STREET?

Diagram showing the portion of Keele street between Weston road and the Grand Trunk right-of-way under the new Toronto Suburban entrance plans and over which a sharp controversy is threatened. The Canadian National Railways contend that the old town of West Toronto consented to the closing of that portion of the street when the agreement to facilitate the laying of sidings for the Union stock yards was made in October, 1903. The agreement, however, was never carried out.

GIVE JAIL TERMS TO ALL MOTORISTS FOUND NEGLIGENT

Time Has Come to Deal Severely, Says Judge Coatsworth

NUMBER INCREASING

The need for drastic steps to be taken to stop the ever growing number of accidents caused by automobiles was the keynote of the address made by Judge Coatsworth to-day to the grand jury at the opening of the general session of the peace for the county of York.

"The time has come," he said, "when we will have to deal very convincingly with those convicted of charges of criminal negligence. Cars should be kept under proper control at all times. When accidents happen through cars not being under proper control charges of criminal negligence result.

"There is an increasing number of these cases, and drastic steps will have to be taken to eliminate them. I think that 95 per cent. of the people who drive cars are reasonably careful and cautious and do their best to avoid accidents. The other five per cent., or it may be less than five per cent., are the cause of all the trouble and are continually being brought into court.

"These men should be sent to jail. The time has come when the public will expect us to protect them against the ever increasing number of these accidents. I think the only remedy is to send the offenders to jail. In addition, we ought to have power to suspend their licenses and forbid them to drive for a certain number of years."

EARNINGS WERE $4,900,000 DURING TRUSTEE'S PERIOD

Information on the earnings of the Toronto Niagara Company's local distribution system within the city during the time it was operated by that corporation as trustees for the city, is at last available.

A report has been prepared for the Toronto Hydro-Electric power commission, showing that during the 23 months it was thus operated, including two, during which it was under the control of the city, the total earnings were approximately $4,900,000.

The operating expenses during that period amounted to $2,000,000, leaving $2,900,000 for fixed charges.

While the report shows a loss of about $100,000 for the period, it is pointed out that this is not really a loss, as it is offset by gold notes to the amount of approximately $850,000, which were paid off by the company. These would have had to be met by the city, and therefore, there is actually a gain of $700,000 for the period.

FIRPO-DEMPSEY RADIO

On Friday evening The Star will broadcast a special radio service on the Dempsey-Firpo fight. De-

NO FLAGS TO FLY WHEN THE EMPRESS DOCKS WITH PRINCE

No Exchange of Addresses and No Social Functions Arranged

HE MAY SLIP ASHORE

Lord Renfrew May Transfer to Lord Byng's Yacht Downstream

Special to The Star by a Staff Reporter.

Quebec, Sept. 11.—For eight million Canadians the smiling boy who steps from the Empress of France to-morrow is the Prince of Wales. To official Quebec he is Baron Renfrew.

The secretary of the harbor commission after an exchange of Marconigrams with the secretary of the Prince, has announced that there will be no civic reception, not even an extra flag on the wharf where the Empress will dock. Quebec society has not prepared any social entertainment. If the Prince stays Mayor Samson may drop around and see him, but there will be no exchange of illuminated addresses.

It was expected that the Prince would stay a day here. Now it is said that he may leave as quickly and as quietly as he is to come. At the Chateau Frontenac it is announced that no reservations have been made for the baronial party.

It is conjectured that the Prince may avoid the regular docking. Lord Byng's yacht, the Lady Grey, is cruising about the lower St. Lawrence. The Prince may transfer from the Empress to the Byng boat, which will dock at a private wharf, but at Spencerwood, the lieutenant-governor's residence, it was stated that there was no preparation there for a princely visit.

In the meantime a four-coach special train lies on the C. P. R. siding. It is at the Prince's disposal. He can pull out for the west the moment he arrives, or he can stay in Quebec an hour or two, or spend the whole day here, as was announced. According to C. P. R. officials this special is to be indefinitely scheduled across Canada. It will stop when Lord Renfrew says stop. It will go when he says go.

One official told The Star that from the standpoint of railroad economics and principles it is likely that after running as a special from Quebec to Montreal this four-coach train will fall in behind the regular which leaves Montreal for the west every night, and follow it as a second section. This would mean that the two trains would cross Canada as one unit. If the Prince's special were to run on a special schedule it might mean the holding up of regular passenger and freight traffic.

The Empress of France is due at nine o'clock to-morrow morning.

MOUNTAINS TOPPLED DURING EARTHQUAKE

Three-Fourths of Tokio Houses are Uninhabitable—Many Buried Alive

Associated Press Despatch.

Tokio, Sept. 11.—Probably three-fourths of the houses in Tokio are uninhabitable for while but half of the capital was destroyed the other half was damaged severely.

The thousands who are sleeping out no doubt prefer this, since earthquakes continue, some of them rather sharp.

Arrivals from the Hakone mountains describe the remarkable effect of the earthquakes there where mountains toppled, filling up valleys and burying alive many hundreds of persons.

It will take weeks to dispose of the dead in Tokio and Yokohama and in the surrounding villages that suffered equally with the larger cities. Despite the privations, horrors and damage suffered in Tokio, life here is returning to normal. Rickshaws have reappeared on the streets. Street cars, however, on which the poorer depend, remain on the tracks where they came to a standstill.

YEAST AND ARTIFICIAL LIGHT PUT PEP IN HENS

Diet and Electric Lamps as Aids to the Egg Output

By SCIENCE SERVICE.

Special to The Star.

Milwaukee, Sept. 11.—By using electric lights to increase the feeding periods and putting yeast in the food, Professors A. J. Souba, H. C. Knandel and R. Adams Dutcher, of Indiana University, have succeeded in increasing egg production by white leghorn hens and pullets. Their experiments were described before the Biological Division of the American Chemical Society in session here to-day.

Ten pens forty-five birds each were fed for ten months on wet and dry mash rations, with and without yeast, and with and without artificial light. Practically all groups which received the yeast diet showed gains. Some of these differences between fowls fed with and without yeast were very slight until the feeding period was increased by arti-

MADAME PONAFIDENE,

who reached America from Russia after a series of most try... She is spending a few days in Toronto with Lady Poynter.

PRINCE SHOWS THE BENE... OF VOYAGE ACROSS ...

Tired Look Is Going From His Eyes and He Is E...ing Better — Enjoys Burlesque Sermon... Applauds Songs at Ship's Concert

Special wireless despatch to The Star. Registered in accordance w... Act of Canada.

On Board the Empress of France, Sept. 11.—Five da... already had their effect on the Prince of Wales, who is tra... as Lord Renfrew. The tired look is going from his eyes and... feeling better than he did when he came aboard at So... retired early last night and did not come up for the dance... in the lounge after the concert.

Monday morning found the Empress running throu... The decks were wet with rain and mist and passengers fo... kept indoors.

Lord Renfrew, whose prime purpose on this trip is res... made this largely a day of rest. In the morning, in com... Engineer H. Teare, he made a thorough tour of the engin... chanical works of the ship, taking great interest in what...

After lunch Lord Renfrew spent some time on ... Commander E. Griffiths, R.N.R. While there the fog ... Empress passed quite close to several large icebergs. Bel... sighted.

In the evening a concert was held in the saloon. Si... Davidson was chairman. Lord Renfrew and his party... apparently thoroughly enjoyed the program. As a young m... Sally brought sunshine to the alley, and then, as an en... boy, a great big wonderful boy," no one laughed and... heartily than the royal passenger. A burlesque sermon by... geon, Dr. Drury, on the text: "Sister Susie's sewing shir... was a scream, and Lord Renfrew appreciated the humor in... artistic items on the program were attentively received.

Eligible Daughters Flo... To See the Prince

Dufferin Terrace Like a Rose Show and Champlai... a Matrimonial Mart—Americans There, T... Look Lord Renfrew Over

Special to The Star by a Staff Reporter.

Quebec, Sept. 11.—Quebec is to-day a city that fidgets and blushes with a secret. Everyone, native or visitor, official or in private station is suffering from a prince complex, and yet the Prince of Wales they say is frank, natural, and not complex at all.

This secret visit of the Prince of Wales is a mystery that is better kept in French and English than in American. Visitors from over the border regard the word incognito as a special and particularly resplendent royal title. One said to The Star: "I have seen your King and Queen, but I have never seen your prince. I was at your fair at Toronto and I thought I would run up to Quebec for a few days to look over your prince."

It was impossible to convince him that there is a great difference between the Prince and Baron Renfrew, American and perhaps Canadian democracy cannot understand that subtle distinction. It is hard to find fault with this frank confession of American weakness. If it were possible all Canada would be here to catch a glimpse of this heir apparent, who, once landed, may not be apparent at all.

None the less fem... run official assu... seems to be full o... eligible daughters ... handsome bachelor ... partner in the Brit... ferin Terrace is like... The Place D'Arme... Chateau Frontenac ... de dames. The B... looks like a matrim... Champlain Market l... like a matrimonial m...

It is said that all ... possible stopping ... Prince's route to Ca... of Canadians unsu... incognito or no inc... cannot pass throug... out someone touchin... cure of body or sou... is also a prince cha... pect immunity from... ation. If the Princ... in some chamber of ... will be many a fo... peep through the k... window.

At the moment t... from which to see ... cession seems to be ... Quebec, not Toront... the logical location... may plunge into C... tunnel and never ... reaches his ranch in...

Bobbed Hair Taboo for Eveni... Transformation, Switches ...

Special to The Star by United Press.

New York, Sept. 11.—Girls will be recognized by their ears this season. Bobbed hair is taboo as a style. Transformations and switches are the mode. Blondes in the afternoon may be brunettes in the evening, or if red hair would be more appropriate with the gown, the hair will have an auburn tint.

These facts came to light at the ... senting practically ... country, are in att...

Bobbed hair ma... for sports wear, b... ous attire. But in ... will be met with up... The heads must b... dinner, theatre or ...

Every girl will h... formations—and ... them in the lower ... as grandmother w...

CHAPTER 4

RED 2

4

Norman Ryan is a vicious, dangerous and resourceful thief.
—TORONTO POLICE CHIEF S.J. DICKSON,
NOVEMBER 1, 1921

Hemingway/Callaghan

Ernest Hemingway was born in Oak Park, Illinois, on July 21, 1899. Morley Callaghan was born in Toronto, Ontario, on February 22, 1903.

Both men worked as reporters at the *Toronto Daily Star*. That's where they met. Both spent time in Paris in the 1920s, where they were the principals in one of literature's best-known boxing matches, at which F. Scott Fitzgerald served (poorly) as timekeeper. Both wrote about Red Ryan.

About the boxing match, I won't go into great detail, except to say that the much smaller Callaghan is said to have handled himself very well. About Ryan . . .

Hemingway's first day as a reporter in the newsroom at the *Star* was September 10, 1923, the day Red Ryan and four other convicts broke out of Kingston Penitentiary.

The men set fire to some hay in the prison stables, fully embracing the literal with their choice of smokescreen. They used a homemade ladder to scale the wall, with Ryan bringing up the rear. Before Ryan went up the ladder, he smashed the jail's chief keeper, Matt Walsh, in the head with the handle of a pitchfork.

Hemingway was put on the overnight train to Kingston. Here's how he described the escape on the front page of the next day's *Star*.

> It was at ten o'clock yesterday morning that a great cloud of thick, yellow-white smoke began to pour from the barn just inside the east wall of the penitentiary. It was the thick dense smoke of a burning straw stack and as it rose it cut off the view of the guard standing with his rifle in the watchtower overlooking the burning barn.
>
> Five men, in the gray prison clothes, ran out of the barn toward the twenty-foot, steep wall. One of them carried a long two-by-four in which spikes had been driven at intervals. The fat man carrying the long scantling leaned it against the wall

and a slim kid, his prison cap pulled
down over his eyes, swarmed up it to
the top of the wall. He carried a
length of rope, which he fastened to
the end of the scantling. He made
the rope fast and then slid down the
other side of the wall.

A big husky with a heavy under-
shot jaw followed him over. On his
heels came a little runt who scrambled up the scantling like a monkey.
He was followed by a thick set, ham-
faced man who scrambled awkwardly
over the wall.

Standing at the foot of the scantling while they all went up was a
thick, freckle-faced man whose prison
cap could not hide his flaming head.
It was "Red" Ryan. The others who
had climbed over were Young Brown,
Big Simpson, Runty Bryans and Wyoming
McMullen.

Ryan was already known as Red, but this was the first time
he was called Red Ryan in the press. It appears Hemingway
just made up the nicknames for the other escaped prisoners:
Young Brown, Big Simpson, Runty Bryans and Wyoming
McMullen, who was serving time for robbing a bank in
Wyoming, Ontario.

McMullen apparently hated his nickname, which stuck. Personally, I think he came off pretty well. Wyoming's not a bad nickname, although I don't think it really belongs in front of McMullen. It also doesn't entirely go with his face.

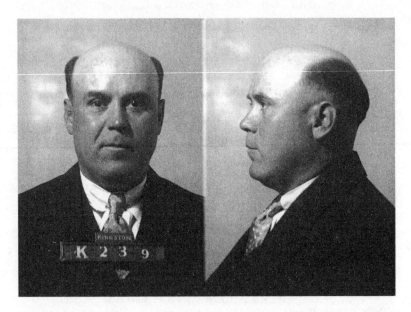

I have no idea how Mr. Bryans felt about Runty, but it seems that he could never catch a break in the nickname department. When he was arrested for a murder in 1938, the *Globe and Mail,* in what was either a mistake or a misprint, wrote that he was also known as Bunty. ("Bad news, boss. The cops got Bunty.")

The jailbreakers scaled the wall, ran across a farmer's field, stole a car and drove off as prison guards fired at them. Wyoming McMullen was driving, and he was hit in the hand. Driving wildly down dirt country roads, he eventually lost control of the car and crashed it into a farm gate, at which point the convicts took off on foot. McMullen had lost a lot of blood, so Ryan carried him into some woods, covered him with cedar boughs, and left him. He was picked up later that day, just a little the worse for wear. The other four spent five days hiding in the swamps and thick bush outside Kingston before hopping a freight train to Belleville and then stealing a car and driving to Toronto.

In Toronto, they needed cash quickly so they could get out of town before someone turned them in for the reward money. But first, Ryan tried a misdirection play, writing a letter to the prison guard he hit with the pitchfork to congratulate him for his bravery, and having a friend mail it from Niagara Falls, New York. Then they picked a bank on the outskirts of Toronto, knocked it over for a little more than three thousand dollars, split the money and took off: Simpson and Bryans to Quebec, Ryan and "Young Brown," whose real name was Arthur "Curly" Sullivan, to Windsor, Ontario, and then across the border to the United States.

According to Roy Greenaway of the *Star,* Ryan and Sullivan crossed the border with sawed-off shotguns under their coats, prepared to use them if they were stopped. According to Peter McSherry, that was just another of Ryan's lies, "puffing up his own legend," and the two were smuggled across the border in a rumrunner's boat.

Either way, Ryan was free. He had a little money in his pocket and a sidekick who did what Ryan told him. And as a result of the Hemingway story and three follow-ups he wrote in Kingston that also ran on the front page, Red Ryan was now very famous. That was the best part.

October–December 1923

Over the next two and a half months, Ryan's reputation as a bank robber was built. According to McSherry, he robbed banks in Chicago; Detroit; Cleveland; St. Paul, Minnesota; and Oshkosh, Wisconsin. He quotes media reports that put the total haul at around $250,000. According to Greenaway, the banks were in Boston, New York, Philadelphia, Pittsburgh and Minneapolis–St. Paul, with a total take of $200,000. Frank Rasky puts all the banks—fourteen of them, by his count—in Michigan, Indiana and Minnesota, and agrees with Greenaway's estimation of the total withdrawal. Rasky also adds a dash of colour, claiming Ryan and his gang threw bombs known as pineapples "at any spectators rude enough to razz their performance." Rasky also says the U.S. press began referring to Ryan as "Canada's Jesse James."

Martin Robin is another popular historian (I'm being generous here to Frank Rasky) who has written about Red Ryan, but unlike most of Ryan's chroniclers, Robin actually did some research. The notes at the back of his book *The Saga of Red Ryan and Other Tales of Violence from Canada's Past* show Robin consulting police archives, reading Royal Commission reports and memoirs, and going through old newspaper records. He says Ryan and Sullivan called themselves the Miller brothers while they were operating in the States. They said they were automobile accessory salesmen. Robin has the boys hitting banks in New York, Philadelphia, Boston and other cities in the east, as well as Flint, Michigan; Fargo, North Dakota; and the Grand

Avenue State Bank in St. Paul. He doesn't speculate how much money was withdrawn.

The St. Paul bank job would have been particularly ballsy. The city operated under what was called the O'Connor Layover Agreement, instituted by police chief John O'Connor. It allowed criminals to stay in the city if they met three conditions: they had to check in with police when they arrived, they had to pay bribes to police and city officials, and they had to agree to commit no crimes in St. Paul. All kinds of gangsters took advantage of the refuge provided by the layover agreement, from John Dillinger and Baby Face Nelson to Ma Barker and her boys. The surrounding communities didn't like it much, but it kept St. Paul pretty much crime free, and the police chief and his cronies well compensated. The agreement lasted until 1935, when a news story about police corruption led to the incarceration or resignation of much of the police force. If Ryan broke the agreement in 1923, he was making some pretty powerful enemies.

But it wasn't St. Paul's finest that did Ryan in, it was his own ego. He just couldn't stop bragging to his friends back home.

Before we get into that, though, here's a little something from the *Toronto Daily Star*'s November 8, 1923, edition. The press coverage of Ryan, never what you would call exceptional in the first place, starts to lose all touch with reality around this time. It's as if his fame gave the papers licence to print whatever the hell they wanted. Ryan would have been in Minnesota when this item appeared.

"RED" RYAN VISITS CITY: GOES ROLLER-SKATING

Norman "Red" Ryan, leader of the bank bandit gang who held up the Bank of Nova Scotia branch, Oakwood and St. Clair, much sought by the Toronto police, is playing hide and seek with the authorities.

It is stated on good authority that Ryan was in Toronto last week, and was seen at a roller rink in company with his sweetheart, a woman well known to the police. The Star was informed Ryan came back to town with his sweetheart to pay a "flying visit" to some friends and stayed the week-end in Toronto.

I suspect that if you could ask Ryan, he would say that those weeks on the run in the United States were the best of his life. The only problem was that all the money, the fast cars it bought, the new clothes, the diamond jewellery, the expensive hotel rooms and restaurants—none of that meant anything to him unless he could tell his friends about it. So he wrote a lot of letters to ex-cons, girlfriends, even inmates still doing time. He also let them know how they could write back to him.

A tip led police to start monitoring the mail going to a girlfriend's mother in Toronto. Eventually, the police learned that the next letter to Ryan was going to the main post office in Minneapolis. A former Toronto chief of detectives and the deputy warden of Kingston headed to Minnesota. After they talked to the chief of the local force, a squad of detectives in civilian clothing was waiting in the post office building when Ryan stopped by to pick up his mail early in the evening of December 14.

The early newspaper accounts of Ryan's capture in Minneapolis are confusing. Initially, they report he was one of four (or five, according to the *Star*) gangsters cornered in the post office; in fact, the *Globe*'s first story about the capture claims they were the same four who escaped together from Kingston. Gradually, however, the reports approached something closer to the truth: that Ryan was alone in the post office and Sullivan was sitting in their car on the street outside.

The police in the post office got the jump on Ryan as he waited in line to pick up his mail. He drew his gun and shot at one of the officers, missing him. A Minneapolis detective shot at Ryan and hit him in his right arm. Ryan's gun fell out of his hand. He tried to make a run for it and was grabbed and cuffed.

As Ryan was being led out of the building, either Sullivan saw him from the car or Ryan called out to him. Sullivan drove off as the detectives began to fire at him. The tip of his nose was hit by one shot. He lost control of his vehicle in the snow, crashed into a parked car and took off on foot, shooting a beat cop as he ran. Eventually, Sullivan got away.

But not for long.

According to the *Star*, under questioning by police, Ryan

gave up the information that Sullivan had a girlfriend in town, a waitress named Irene Adams. The police contacted her, she admitted the relationship, and they were waiting in her apartment the next day when Sullivan knocked on her door. Surprised by the police, Sullivan went for his gun and was shot through the heart.

Ryan was taken to the morgue to identify the body. According to the *Globe*, he gazed at his friend for a full minute with tears welling in his eyes. "That is tough, isn't it? I wish I was with him," he said.

There is some debate over whether Ryan ratted out Sullivan. I suspect he did. I think it would have galled him that he, the famous Red Ryan, the "dapper Toronto bank robber," as the *Star* described him the next day, had been captured, while Curly Sullivan, a nobody whom most of the papers still referred to as Arthur Brown, had escaped. Also, throughout his life, when offered a choice between talking and not talking, Ryan generally picked the former.

Ryan denied it, of course. In an interview with a *Star* reporter a couple of weeks later, after the Toronto papers reported that he had "squealed" on Sullivan, Ryan said, "Toronto is my home, my relatives live here. They have suffered enough through my actions and to couple the name of Ryan with a squealer is contemptible. I may be a bank robber—and it is true my record as such is a black one, yet I never gave a pal away in my life. Sullivan and I stuck together after we left Toronto and to say I did him dirt is stabbing a man in the back."

Frank Rasky had no doubt that Ryan turned Sullivan in. For some reason Rasky refers to Sullivan throughout his

Harlequin story as "Peanut-head." He has Ryan say to the cops right after his arrest, "You'll find Peanut-head hiding in his gun moll's apartment uptown." And then later, after hearing that Sullivan had been killed, Rasky quotes Ryan as saying, "Poor guy. His peanut head got separated from his hat." It's probably unnecessary to point out that Rasky's thoughts regarding quotation marks and their proper usage may not have been quite in line with the way we view these things today. They were, however, remarkably in line with those of the reporters working for Canada's major newspapers in the 1920s.

On page 5 of the December 20, 1923, edition of the *Globe*, it was reported that police officials in Minneapolis were amused by the "many and varied 'interviews' and 'confessions' which are being credited to their prisoner, 'Red' Ryan, in newspaper reports." Apparently, apart from the grilling he was given by Minneapolis and Canadian police, he had said practically nothing during his captivity.

I don't know what *Globe* readers were supposed to take away from this. I suppose that would depend on how good their memories were, because three days earlier, on December 17, the very same *Globe*'s front page had featured an "interview" with Ryan under the headline "Bandit Leader Weeps When He Views Body of Slain Companion." The first paragraph reads:

> "It was the woman who did it,"
> declared "Red" Ryan, escaped convict
> tonight, in discussing his capture
> in Minneapolis Friday night, and the

subsequent killing of his pal, Arthur
Brown (alias Sullivan), by a detective on Saturday afternoon. "Brown
always had a failing for women, and
I warned him against it. I learned
the lesson long ago that you can't
get too friendly with women when you
are wanted. They'll turn you up every
time."

Either the reporter made the whole thing up, or Ryan got his
partner's last name wrong (Brown was the alias, not Sullivan)
and was also a little confused about his own hometown: "I
grew up around Detroit," he said, "and the gang I trained with
was not any too quiet."

Ryan also wasn't shy about writing his ticket to a U.S.
prison:

"We were in the Twin Cities off and
on, making trips east, but did not
turn a trick until about six weeks
ago, when we stuck up the bank in
St. Paul. We got five thousand dollars
out of that job, but most of it is
gone now.

"We picked up a car near St. Paul
for the bank job. I don't know what
make it was. That never made any difference. We've had plenty of them in

our time, and left them all in the
ditch when we were through with them."

Tough on cars, but a gentleman, nonetheless: "No, we didn't
rob any of the customers in the St. Paul bank. I never rob
women."

The reporters in Minneapolis, under pressure from their
editors, were simply making stuff up. There was a question-and-
answer interrogation session between Ryan and a detective
that ran in the *Star* on December 17. An interesting "yarn"

A LITTLE MORE RASKY

Ryan teamed up with another bank special-
ist, Andy ("Peanut-head") Sullivan, a thin
long-nosed convict. Ryan was dubious whether
Peanut-head was skilled enough to heist banks,
and he taunted him. "You're a trellis for vari-
cose veins," Red jeered at him. "Your nose is
so long, you're the only guy who can take a
shower and smoke a cigar at the same time. I'm
sure they put better heads on umbrellas."

Rasky writes Red Ryan as if he's a comedian playing the
Catskills. I mentioned that Rasky had made up the Peanut-head
nickname, but "heist" as a verb? That's gold. Say it like "hoist"
and you return the word to its place of birth.

on the 18th that included Ryan's thoughts on the "dope fiends" in Kingston and how the dope came over the walls of the prison at night. A "vivid story" told by Ryan to an unnamed reporter all about his escape from Kingston and his "subsequent escapades." A story the same week in which he describes asking a woman with a baby carriage to wait outside a bank in Cleveland while he robbed it. A story supposedly told by Minneapolis detectives to "illustrate the cunningness of Ryan" in which he is stripped and searched before being given jail clothes and put in his cell. An hour later, Ryan "carelessly" hands the jailer a twenty-dollar bill and asks him to bring him a chicken dinner. There was a cryptic story involving a French convict, coded letters and the death of a young woman in England, said to be "one of the dark chapters of Ryan's overseas experience." A story that "intimates" of Ryan had over $200,000 stashed somewhere. And an explosive scene between Ryan and Sullivan's widow, fully fleshed out with all the melodrama you'd expect:

> "You are a cheap crook, and always had women following you around," said Mrs. Sullivan with pent up anger, when Ryan greeted her entrance to the cells with a grin of familiarity.
>
> "You are to blame for all my trouble. You are the one that led my husband into the crimes, and you are the one that got him killed; you

```
betrayed him; you who posed as his
friend," she went on.
     Ryan took on a harder expression.
     "No, not me. I did not turn my old
pal up. It was the 'skirt' that gave
him away, just as I always told him
they would," he replied.
```

Ryan was asked later about that last story. With moist eyes and a deep sigh he said Mrs. Sullivan was as nice as could be when they met. There wasn't a harsh word exchanged between the two. Which, of course, could just be shit of a different colour.

January 4–8, 1924

But here's something that wasn't made up. Freezing in his cold cell, Ryan asked his jailers to go to his hotel and bring him his overcoat, which they did. He also started to fight against his extradition to Canada, instructing his lawyers to initiate the long process of serving out a writ of habeas corpus in a Minnesota district court and confessing to a string of unsolved robberies in the United States.

On January 4, after Ryan had been transferred to a county jail to answer a deportation warrant, it became clear why he was stalling his return trip to Canada. Two of the bars in his cell had been sawn almost clean through; they just needed a strong pull to break them off. A handmade rope ladder of twisted underwear, clothing and strips of blanket was hidden under his bed. The overcoat he asked for had

had a piece of hacksaw blade sewn into the hem. Ryan had spent the past three weeks sawing bars every night. Once his plan was discovered, he stopped stalling and signed a waiver that put his deportation order into immediate effect. He was on a train to Toronto that afternoon.

He said later if he had had just one more night in the cell, he would have been gone.

Red Ryan made the Sunday *New York Times* on January 6. It's a small item on page 4, under a Minneapolis dateline.

> Norman ("Red") Ryan, bank bandit and gunman, who boasted that he never would be returned to Canada alive, was turned over to the custody of Canadian officials and, under a heavy guard, crossed the boundary line this morning. He was captured a month ago in a gun fight here in which a patrolman was wounded and Ryan was shot in the shoulder.

In the four days it took Ryan to get from the U.S. border to Kingston Penitentiary's dungeon, we are told the following happened:

1. On the train back to Toronto, according to the *Star* reporter who was allowed to board and ride with Ryan, he "acted as if he were a schoolboy going

home for a holiday. . . . [F]or hours he laughed and joked, interchanged wise-cracks with his captors, reminisced, and chatted."

2. At Toronto's Don Jail, after stripping, undergoing a full body search by the guards and showering, Ryan pulled a prank. This was widely reported and became a centrepiece of the Red Ryan legend. Even his biographer McSherry mentions it without his usual clear-eyed qualifications. None of that makes it any easier to believe. I like to imagine it as a scene from a thirties prison flick, with Gary Cooper as "Red."

INTERIOR: CELL BLOCK: DAY

The warden strolls slowly past the cells of the inmates, looking each man up and down. "Red" is leaning against his cell door. He has a mischievous grin.

RED: Say, Warden, how would you like to see a good trick?
WARDEN: What kind of trick, Red?

The guards with the warden start elbowing each other. Old Red's up to something.

RED: Well, I'll show you . . . in return for a steak dinner.

The guards crack up at this. The warden quiets them with a glance.

WARDEN: A steak dinner, eh? Steak's pretty expensive, Red. How do I know your trick's worth a steak dinner?

Red's eyes twinkle and his smile gets bigger as he slowly pulls a seven-inch-long hacksaw blade out of his shirt pocket. He hands it to the wide-eyed warden.

WARDEN: *(Regaining his composure and starting to chuckle)* Well, I'll be! That sure is a swell trick, Red. *(To the guards, who are barely controlling their laughter)* Boys, pick out the thickest steak we've got and fry it up for Red Ryan!
RED: And remember . . . I like 'em rare!

Laughter and back-slapping all around.

That's pretty much how the *Star* wrote it up, in a story illustrated with a picture of a hacksaw blade. The story quotes Ryan as saying, "I got a lovely juicy steak."

He said he smuggled the saw blade into the jail stuck to the bottom of his foot with "sticking gum." When he realized that he wasn't going to be left alone, unwatched, in his cell, and also that his leg shackles weren't coming off, he decided to turn it over. "I knew I was finished. . . . So what was the use?" When the reporter expressed skepticism about the story, Ryan insisted it was true. "It is no kid—I did it."

3. After declaring his intention to fight the charges against him related to the Toronto bank robbery the four fugitives had taken part in to fund their escape, Ryan and his entourage headed to Union Station to catch the train to Kingston. But they were intercepted by Ryan's brother Frank, who asked to speak

to Red alone. They talked as the police watched from a distance. Frank waved his arms in the air. He waved a piece of paper in the air. He was trying to convince Red of something. Apparently he succeeded, because after the talk ended, Ryan told his guards he'd changed his mind; he was pleading guilty. So the whole gang did a U-turn and headed back to court.

Two hours later, after receiving a sentence of life in prison and thirty lashes, Ryan was on his way back to the train station and Kingston, but this time he wasn't going to await trial, he was going for the rest of his life.

Various theories were floated about the reason for Ryan's change of mind. Some speculated he wanted to spare his family the embarrassment of a long trial. The *Globe* wondered if one of Ryan's relatives would have been implicated as the getaway driver in the bank job.

One thing is certain, justice sure happened quick in 1924.

Needless to say, all this was covered breathlessly, moment by moment, on the front pages of all the Toronto papers. There were pictures of Ryan in cuffs and shackles, standing next to the detectives who brought him back. Ryan's wedding photos were published, as were pictures of Ryan's "arsenal": his guns, bullets, carrying cases "in which the gang transported the loot from their daring hold-ups" and a shot of the homemade rope ladder found in his Minneapolis jail cell.

The *Star* even printed a little boxed-off sidebar story next to its coverage of Ryan in court. Under the headline "First Downfall Was Apple Tree," an unnamed relative speculated that Red's life of crime was probably caused by a fall out of an apple tree when he was a young boy. "Something must have happened then," the relative said. "He hasn't been right since."

It was during these days that the *Star*'s coverage of Ryan began to distance itself from the other dailies, not in the quality of its journalism, but in enthusiasm, effort and panache. The paper had placed a reporter on the train from Minneapolis with Ryan, giving readers the first legitimate interview with him since his arrest. This piece, written by A.L. McIntyre, established the generous, almost fawning tone that the *Star* would use with Ryan from now on. Consider this:

```
He has no criminal face. His features
are well formed. His eyes are steady.
He smiles readily, a winning smile,
revealing white even teeth.
```

And:

```
He has the build of an athlete.
Photographs haven't shown this. For
pictures have shown him handcuffed,
with his wrists drawn together, with
shoulders hunched, giving him a thin
appearance. But when the cuffs are off
he throws his shoulders back and the
```

proportion is just right for his six
feet of height and his hundred and
eighty pounds of weight.

Not everyone was a fan of this style of coverage. Inspector William Wallace, the assistant chief of detectives for the city of Toronto, wrote an article for the *Canadian Police Bulletin* entitled "Red Ryan Only a Plaster Hero" in which he took very strong exception to the pedestal being built for Ryan by the press. Wallace wrote that Ryan was not just a failure as a man, he wasn't even much of a crook.

Ryan, as a criminal, was never possessed of either the courage or
resourcefulness to become more than
a common thief, viciously inclined.
What has this poor fellow ever done
to lift his criminal career above
the commonplace? What act has he ever
performed that would indicate that
he was either brave or ingenious?
Once he was granted parole on the
understanding that he would go to
France and fight for his country. He
went part of the way and did all in
his power to disgrace his comrades
and the land of his birth. Finally
he assaulted and robbed an Australian
marine of his credentials, assumed the

name of his victim, got to the other end of the world and remained at long range until the clouds rolled by.

We are told that Ryan married a young girl and subsequently threw her aside. It has been told by one who should know, that a little horseplay took place in Minneapolis that sent Ryan almost to his knees whining like a whipped cur for mercy—mercy is a word that had passed out of his vocabulary years before and was only recalled to his memory for the protection of his own hide.

Ryan, although still in the prime of manhood, is a dejected wretch, paying the price of his indolence and uncurbed evil desires. No young man can follow Ryan's example without sooner or later meeting with a similar fate.

But it appears Wallace's was a lonely voice. The public couldn't get enough of Ryan.

The *Star* assigned a reporter named Athol Gow to the Ryan beat. Gow had grown up in Ryan's neighbourhood, and the two had known each other since boyhood. When Ryan boarded the train to Kingston, Gow got on with him, sending back quotes like this one, directed at the youth of Toronto:

"Tell them for me to keep on life's straight and narrow path. The criminal life does not pay." It was a theme Ryan would come back to.

On January 8, the day Ryan was being processed at Kingston Penitentiary, the *Star* reported that "'Red' Ryan's long career of crime is over."

In the next day's edition, Athol Gow's inside report of that processing ran. Gow was allowed to follow Ryan into the registration room, watch as he was strip-searched, his hair combed through, the soles of his feet checked. The final line of Gow's report, after he watched Ryan walk through the door leading from the registration room to the dungeon, and after hearing the dungeon door clang shut, is "Exit Norman Red Ryan."

If it all ended here, the Red Ryan story would be much of a piece with those of the other gangsters of the era, the only difference being that Ryan's story wouldn't have ended with a picture of his bullet-riddled corpse. But it didn't end here.

It was about to get biblical.

CHAPTER 5

BASED ON A TRUE STORY

5

I know a guy who ghost-wrote the autobiography of one of the most famous and well-loved Canadians of the twentieth century. It was a pure ghost job. He didn't get a "with." So, as far as readers and future researchers are concerned, this book came straight from the source. I don't know what kind of confidentiality agreement he had with the publisher, so I'll be purposely vague here. I don't want to bring him any grief.

His subject was very near death and was physically unable to take on any role in the project. Also, the subject was not what you would describe as an introspective chronicler of his or her own life (vagueness), so there was no vast, authoritative written record of events. What there was were old stories, often repeated, the reminiscences of others, previous biographies and press clippings. So here's how it worked. Where my friend saw two different versions of a story, it was up to him to decide which one would go into the history books as the true version. Where there were no details or colour, he made up details and colour. Some of the events in the book he just simply invented.

I'm not condemning this. Far from it. I think it's very likely that the same thing can be said of most autobiographies, even the ones actually written by the person whose picture is on the cover. All I'm saying is, it's all just stories. Fact. Fiction. Serious journalism. Gutter journalism. History. It's all just stories.

Over the course of this work, I've found myself thinking more and more about the relationship between information and the truth, and about how a lot of the problems we find ourselves dealing with these days flow from a confusion we seem to have about the two concepts.

Information, data—even facts, for that matter—are not truth. Facts can sometimes get you closer to the truth, but they just as often get in the way. Peter McSherry chased down a lot of facts over the twenty-odd years he spent working on his Ryan book. Others, like Martin Robin, had Ryan born on Markham Street, but McSherry showed in great detail how that was not the case. He was able to prove conclusively that Ryan was born on Esther Street, a few blocks to the east. That's a fact. But I don't particularly care about it, just as I don't particularly care when McSherry gets a fact wrong. For example (and this is jumping ahead in the narrative, I know), he has Ryan beginning his job selling cars at Fawcett Motors in late

January 1936. But I have a copy of the *Star* with a Fawcett Motors ad featuring Ryan from August 1935. Wrong fact.

But here's the thing: most of the newspaper stories about Ryan were filled with "facts," both right and wrong. Laced with them. Newspaper readers in the 1920s and '30s were given a lot of information about Red Ryan, but almost no truth. We can see that clearly in hindsight, but why wasn't it also clear in the moment? Wouldn't the application of judgment to the facts being presented have exposed the charade back then? Why couldn't people see then that a combination of interests—political, commercial and personal—was about to lead to disaster?

A couple of pages after McSherry messed up the starting date of Ryan's job selling cars, he wrote something that wasn't based on fact but that seems to me to have the ring of truth. After stating that, in October 1935, Ryan returned to his life of crime, he wrote, "He never intended otherwise."

That is a truth McSherry came to in a different way than the way he tracked down the street of Ryan's birthplace. It's a result of the thousands of hours he spent researching Ryan, but not in the same sense that the unearthing of a specific detail is. McSherry has come to an understanding about Ryan, he has achieved an empathy that allowed him to write something true in a much more profound sense.

That is a truth that doesn't require a qualifier, because McSherry feels it to be true. One doesn't often come across this kind of truth in journalism. It is, perhaps, what the filmmaker Werner Herzog would describe as an "ecstatic" truth.

In 1999, Herzog wrote a manifesto he called "Lessons

of Darkness," which has come to be called the Minnesota Declaration, a set of twelve principles about truth and fact in documentary cinema. The manifesto is a declaration of war against cinéma-vérité.

I've never heard the case for a consideration of Herzog's ideas in journalism, but I think reporters of a certain mindset will experience some self-recognition reading his description of cinéma-vérité as "the truth of accountants."

"It reaches a merely superficial truth," writes Herzog.

He says cinéma-vérité confuses facts with truth, and therefore "ploughs only stones." And he goes on, "There are deeper strata of truth in cinema, and there is such a thing as poetic, ecstatic truth. It is mysterious and elusive, and can be reached only through fabrication and imagination and stylization."

Facts vs. truth. Truth vs. information.

This is a lesson with a certain amount of urgency today, given the much larger mountains of information available to us now, and given our recent issues with truth.

Determining the truth is not just a matter of amassing all the information that's available to you. That just leads to overload, confusion and petty squabbles over details. It also leads to people thinking truth isn't that important because there's simply too much information to cope with, and that information doesn't always fit neatly together. And when truth stops being important, we end up with the mess we see around us now.

If you care about truth, it's important to separate the idea of truth from the image of an endless stream of information no one can possibly master.

Truth is something else.

Truth isn't just knowing all the facts; it is being able to evaluate what's presented to you and being able to determine whether those things you're being told actually square with what you know about reality, or with what you can find out through informed sources about the nature of reality.

Consideration and judgment are required to turn data into truth. And we are not particularly good at consideration and judgment. We weren't good at it back when Ontario's pet boy was on the front page and, if anything, we're worse at it today, now that consideration consists chiefly of hitching your wagon to a particular team, and judgment is manifested as an endless stream of likes and retweets.

And as tough as truth is, getting deeper than truth, getting to where Herzog wants to take us, is more difficult still. Because on top of consideration and judgment, that journey requires empathy. Informed empathy. Without that, the fabrication Herzog writes about is just lying, and the stylization is just glitter.

Ecstatic truth is an elusive goal, and in anticipation of not getting there, I thought I should at least write a manifesto. So here's my declaration for this project. Here is my justification for all the lies and all the glitter:

1. I refuse to let the truth stand in the way of a good story.
2. If the myth is more interesting than the facts, I'm going with the myth, or at least giving it equal billing. This whole story is a tug-of-war between fact and fiction, and sometimes fiction pulls harder.

3. If you find yourself wondering what to believe, or wondering where I'm going next, please be reassured by the knowledge that I don't know either.

4. If, as per the Minnesota Declaration, facts create norms and truth creates illumination, then fact-checking this book would clearly be a waste of time and money.

5. Based on the "fact" that Frank Rasky was a former crime reporter for the *Vancouver Sun,* the Red Ryan chapter of *Gay Canadian Rogues* (Harlequin, 1958) shall be considered journalism.

6. The information I have is good enough. Sure, there's more out there. I don't have many clippings from the *Telegram,* for example, and none at all from the *Mail.* But all in all, I'd rather have Rasky.

Extra Bonus Principle: This book will contain indispensable tips for turning the Red Ryan story into a first-class, 1930s-style Hollywood biopic, more than worthy of the Tinseltown stamp of legitimacy: "Based on a True Story."

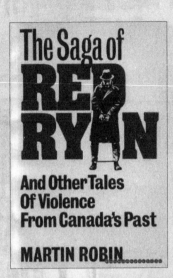

Martin Robin wrote *The Saga of Red Ryan and Other Tales of Violence from Canada's Past* in 1982. There are six stories contained in it, a "collection of rogues and victims," as the jacket blurb puts it, and I think it's quite safe to say that Ryan would have been very happy to know that, forty-six years after his death, he was still the headliner.

The front cover photo is worth more than a glance. It's a shot of Ryan in handcuffs and leg irons, taken by a *Star* photographer upon Ryan's return to Toronto after his capture in Minnesota in early 1924. But while the original newspaper image shows Ryan's legs close together and catches him taking the tiny steps the leg irons allow, the cover image—in a kind of proto-Photoshop—has his legs spread wide, wider than his shoulders, and the chain between his ankles stretched tight. He becomes, with this simple cut-and-paste, much more powerful and threatening, and the new image acquires a kind of ecstatic truth that's missing from the original. I think Ryan would have appreciated it.

That his wider legs and the stretched chain also form the capital *A* in his last name is, as far as I'm concerned anyway, simply a happy graphic coincidence.

Listens in to Moth; Cost Rises in Pool; Paris Suburbs

This is the American embassy in Tokio, three months after the earthquake and fire. The tents used by the marine guard and members of the staff, who are taking no chances with heavier building materials.

Mlle. Christianne Fournier has written a book called "Adam, Eve and the Serpent," in which she describes life as seen by the university student in Paris. For this she has received the Professional Liberals' first winter prize.

Again history repeats itself. The Paris suburbs are on the Seine. It is believed that the floods will rise above estimated in millions.

When the S.S. Mahalla docked in New York city, it was learned that she had on board sea-door cadets from the British Isles, who are working and studying on the ship the idea that they may own vessels of their own some day.

This is ski-jumping time. Already the long gliders have made their appearance on the Canadian slopes, whether natural or artificial.

Norman "Red" Ryan, notorious Canadian bank bandit, was carefully sealed and delivered to the authorities on this side from Minneapolis, where he was captured. He is shown, shackled and hand-cuffed, arriving in Toronto with Inspector Duncan.

Her stunts are the envy of others several times her age. With the cold weather and ice on the ponds and open spaces, Canadian youth is given an opportunity to try out the skates. Santa left.

Still hungry! These three German boys have just received their rations from the kitchens of a relief organization—but still, by scraping the soup kettles carefully, they have hopes of finding something left.

This is the latest photograph of France's Olympic pool as it looks to-day. It was to cost 10,000 but it has been found that on completion it cost million.

Five-year-old Parisian prodigy, Pietro Mazzini, already plays and Mozart as well as his own compositions, series of concerts in Vienna, he is to sail for this continent, with his mother, for engagements here.

Without the consent or knowledge of his mother, Harry Kendall Thaw has been conferring with lawyers in an effort to obtain his release from the Philadelphia Insane Asylum, on the ground that he is a sane man.

Eleanor Coleman, of Milwaukee, woman's world champion for the hundred-yard breast stroke, successfully defended her title at a swimming meet in Chicago recently.

Dr. Phillips Thomas, Westinghouse research engineer, using the ultra audible microphone recently invented, determines if sound communication can be heard by ear. He is listening in to the moth.

CHAPTER
6

POETIC TRUTH

6

——

Can we consider together the possibility that the truth we are seeking can be found in poetry? You see, I haven't mentioned it before, but Red Ryan was a poet. Published.

Now, that claim isn't without controversy, so let me lay out the facts.

After Ryan was picked up in Minneapolis in December 1923, while he was stalling his return to Canada during the day and sawing away at the bars of his cell window during the night, he retained the services of a lawyer based in Hamilton, Ontario, to defend him against bank robbery charges in Toronto, just in case his deportation fight failed. In exchange for representing Ryan, the lawyer, C.S. Morgan, asked Ryan to agree to cooperate in the publication of a book about his life. Ryan, of course, agreed.

That book was called *"Red" Ryan's Rhymes and Episodes,* and it is, as the title suggests, a combination of biographical sketches and poems. Only one writer is credited on the front cover: Norman J. Ryan. This book is the source of the Ryan quotes I used to pad out chapter 1.

Peter McSherry didn't buy it. He described the book as combining "a few of Red Ryan's reminiscences with much of Morgan's fertile imagination and Morgan's own high school poetry," and if McSherry was able to obtain a copy of the book, which is extremely hard to find, there is no evidence of it in his work. No quotes from any of the rhymes. No quotes from any of the episodes.

The editor's note at the beginning of the book would seem to back up McSherry's assertion, at least as far as the poems go.

The rhymes in this book are written from information obtained from interviews with Norman J. Ryan and others. The episodes are written as nearly as possible word for word from the author's narrative.

But I would like to propose another way of looking at that editor's note.

We tend to think of non-fiction and fiction as operating on mutually exclusive frequencies, the one literal and objective, the other figurative and subjective. It is the classic-versus-romantic debate once again, pitting the clear and unadorned against the obscure and symbolic. They are the two extreme end points of the writing continuum. If we were to try to fit poetry into this figuration, the tendency would be to extend the continuum on the fiction side and place poetry even further away from non-fiction, further from what we consider to be the objective truth. But perhaps Ryan knew better. Perhaps Ryan saw poetry secretly circling back around to take on non-fiction's job. Perhaps he saw the potential to reach, through poetry, a deeper, more profound "poetic truth."

For a man who spent his entire adult life creating the public persona of Red Ryan—the bluff, daring man of action who betrayed no fears or doubts—the prospect of his poetry stripping all that away and leaving him emotionally and intellectually naked on the public stage must have been terrifying. Wouldn't he have insisted that his verses be credited to an editor?

There's also the fact that Ryan knew he was heading back to prison for a very long time, and probably didn't look forward to spending the rest of his life hearing his toothless, smirking cellmates begin every conversation with him by saying, "Hey, Shakespeare."

So taking all that into consideration, and reminding you of the first point in my project manifesto, I therefore declare Red Ryan to be a poet.

Now that that's settled, let's read some poems.

There are eight in the collection. The first, called "Ostracized," delivers its "don't judge a book by its cover" message by contrasting the life of the convict ("His close shorn hair, his careworn face, / His worn attire, his awkward grace") with those of the belles of "gay society" ("who paint your faces, rouge your lips, / Who ride in parlor cars and sail in ships"). But while the life of the jailbird is a hard one, reward comes at the end, when

> *The debt now paid in full, he's bought his soul.*
> *He's gentle and he's kind, for he has sought*
> *The wisdom that no wealth has ever bought.*

Whereas, for the painted ladies of luxury, no such ultimate reward awaits: "You have what wealth can buy, / But have you strength to bear your cross when you lay down and die?"

It certainly makes you think.

The second rhyme is called "Daylight and Darkness" and, as the title suggests, the technique of contrast, employed so successfully in the first poem, is again used here. We are given two settings to contemplate: nature ("Where the tall trees grow and the rivers run, / Where the fields are kissed by the golden sun") and prison ("Where the cells are cold and locked up tight, / Where weird sounds travail through the night"). The contrast is a stark one, as is the effect on a person. God is in nature ("For standing there I heard a Voice"), as is balm for the "cankered starving soul." No such balm exists in jail, that most unnatural of environments, "Where your thoughts are locked in bands of steel."

It concludes with these thoughts on prison. Maybe Ryan was reflecting on his days in the Pen, pictured on the facing page. (He's the second pair of white pants standing from the left.)

There's sorrow here and much lament,
And little treasure ever sent.
Bring here your soul so full of sin,
They'll build a box to put you in.

Standard Cell - Kingston Aug. 1928

Would it be unfair to point out a slight disconnect with the message of poem number one?

With the third rhyme we come to a real change of pace, an Irish drinking song of a poem, complete with internal rhymes within the lines, called "We Hold-Up Men." It begins, "Now and then we hold-up men shake down a cushy lay. / With an empty gat we hang our hat where tellers work all day." Regular crossword solvers will know "gat" is early twentieth-century gangster slang for "gun." The fact that it's described as being empty is consistent with a line of BS Ryan regularly peddled, claiming he robbed banks with an empty gun, so that no employees or customers were ever in danger.

This poem's a good bit of fun. Ryan slags the police for incompetence and bankers for their cold-heartedness. My favourite stanza is the second:

A hold-up man I've been, I am, I walk right in the door,
Pull down my hat and flash my gat and lay them on the floor.
And then I say in kindest tones "Just pack my canvas bag,"
And then I saunter out again and with me comes the swag.

Next up is a piece in the Robert Service style called "The Rendezvous." It's a bit of social commentary set in a bar with a bunch of crooks bragging about the jobs they've pulled. The gangster slang Ryan uses to describe his fellow drinkers is priceless: "The man on my right was a well mugged yegg, the man on my left a stool." Another is called a "dip." But the prize goes to the last one:

The gink at my side was "Old Woe Betide."
His tongue pattered thick and loose.
He drowned his sorrows and gay to-morrows in swallows of
  thick corn juice.

A yegg, a stool, a dip and a gink. "Stool," obviously, meant stool pigeon. A "yegg" was a burglar or a safecracker. "Dip" was a pejorative term for pickpockets who didn't possess enough skill to rightly be called pickpockets. And "gink," as far as I can figure out, just meant an oddball or a fool.

But beyond the names, the poem contains a serious message: that the primary driver of crime is poverty.

The grim spectre poverty knocks at the door,
Necessity mothers the deed,
We know how they feel when they go out and steal
The things that the children may need.

This line of thinking wasn't exactly groundbreaking in the 1920s, but it was considerably more progressive than most lines of thinking at the time. As was the thought that closes the poem:

It's the bull and his bracelets that robs us of pride,
It's the sting of the cell that we feel.
We are bagged and then tagged till all hope has now died
And they won't give us work so we steal.

This is Red Ryan as social justice crusader. In my reading, "the bull and his bracelets" refers to a captive wild thing, the bracelets being the nose rings used to confine the animal. Or I might be overthinking things and he's just referring to a cop with handcuffs. And while the setup might be a little clumsy, you've got to agree that last line is pretty damn good.

Really, the less said about poem number five, "Up and Down," the better.

But the next rhyme more than makes up for it. It's a wild, cocaine-fuelled ride to oblivion called "The Song of the Snow Bird." It begins: "Ring-a-round a rosey, our Jim is snuffed with snow, / He's climbed the golden ladder now where all the fairies go." Reading this, you think the opening is too strong; there's no way he'll be able to keep up the pace. But he does, and then some: "He copped a rock that flickered just like the twinkling stars, / That's why he's sniffed his way to-night to sit up late with Mars."

Poor Jim has two big problems: he loves his cocaine, and he's married to a classic enabler.

> *She took her knife and cut a deck from out behind a seam,*
> *Then took a match and warmed a pan that sent him in a*
>   *dream;*
> *He smiled, and staggered to his feet, and thanked her then and*
>   *there,*
> *And then he took another sniff and climbed the golden stair.*

Seriously, check this out:

> *Oh, listen to the birdies sing, the clouds go rolling by,*
> *He sees the silver linings now, how fast they multiply;*

He's gone back home to mother, he holds her gentle hand,
He's sniffed his way another day into the promised land.

I'm left with one very big question after reading this poem: When we consider the influence of twentieth-century drug culture on literature, why is Ryan's name never mentioned?

Read one way, the next poem, "The Lawyer," could be seen as proof that McSherry was right, and old C.S. Morgan really did write these poems himself. It's a paean to defence attorneys, who may not always win, but when they lose, shake your hand with a tear in their eye, because that guilty verdict hurts them more than it hurts you. The poem ends with the jailbird lying in bed in his cell, dreaming of "that wonderful fight" his lawyer put up in court and vowing to send for him again, the next time he needs "a good mouth-piece."

Read another way, "The Lawyer" is a very bad poem.

In the final poem we encounter, at last, Red Ryan's poetic truth. It's his masterpiece, "Solitary." This one deserves to be reproduced in full.

SOLITARY

The solitary cell is hell, it takes away your mind.
They say that it is chastening to all of human kind.
It may be so, but I think not, for squatting in this hole
I see grim spectres, awful sights that try to steal my soul.
My body do with what you will, but leave my soul to me,
I know you have a heart of stone lacking sympathy.

There is a peep hole in the door, where I look with one eye,
I wonder if you're leaving me to rot away and die.

Each minute seems just like an hour, each hour like many years;
I wonder if you'd take my place and wipe away my tears.
Oh men of strength and worldly poise, you know not what you do,
You've done this awful thing to me and many others too.

You say that I'm a sinner. I say to you it's true,
The things I've done, never a one that I again will do.
My soul has been in torture and my head is now in pain,
Unlock the door and take me out, don't bring me back again.

There is a peep hole in the door. The world is far away,
I don't know how long I've been here, but now I kneel and pray,
I see ten thousand demons gathered all around the floor,
If you believe there is a God, oh please unlock the door.

This is a heart-wrenching cry for mercy, full of grim spectres and "ten thousand demons," from a flawed man who fears the loss of his soul. It's also a powerful moral condemnation of the inhumanity of solitary confinement, a message with a great deal of resonance today.

This is the poem that Ryan—ultimately—couldn't allow the world to believe was written by him.

The Justice Department was unsuccessfully petitioned in 1924 to prevent the publication of *"Red" Ryan's Rhymes and Episodes* by a group Martin Robin described as "the aroused executive of the Women's Christian Temperance Union." I'm not sure if the sauciness was intentional. McSherry said the book outraged church and civic groups right across the country. But poetry has always been an acquired taste.

WHERE FIRE WAS STARTED

"CIGARETTE PAPER" MUTINY IS QUELLED IN KINGSTON

Above is seen a general view of Portsmouth penitentiary, outside Kingston, Ont., which was the scene of a serious uprising of prisoners on Monday. The fact that they were not given cigarette papers with which to smoke their prison tobacco rations was cited by recently-released inmates as one of the chief grievances of the prisoners. This, and confinement in "the hole," or solitary confinement, as punishment, are said by these "outsiders" to have led to the outbreak, which was only quelled after military units were called in from Kingston. A number of inmates of the penitentiary, who achieved prominence at the time of their conviction and sentence, are shown: (1) "Tim" Buck, former leading member of the Communist party of Canada; (2) "Two-gun" O'Brien, armed robber; (4) "Red" Ryan; (5) Sydney Lass, payroll robber; (6) Wm. McMullen, armed robber.

D WITH HOSE SAYS CLARK

Murder Sooner ...ke It," He ...clares

...RD DEGREE

...ark, alias Williams ...udge Field, charged ...violence, was ques... regard to a state... after his arrest ...signed it in a ...lid police officer with ...Clark said Detec... struck him in the ...ring the hose and ...rith it. The pris... rt he had received ... "twice before and ...ign for murder ...nother beating.

...harles B. Neal on ...attacked George ...oy, while he was ...on Oriole Rd. on

...giving evidence in ...old of being at his ... p.m. He recalled ...because he wished ... that night regard... his mother of a ...she had been given

...reated Aug. 22 by ...d two other offi...

...he was remanded ...a week and sent ...pen."

...tectives, by the ...ok me to his room ...ross the face with ...nd," said witness, ...view at which his ...had been taken.

...at With Hose ...d came back with ...a piece of hose ...d, "and told me ...he would give me ... given Campbell," ...ee, for assault ...k?" "No, I never

...at this statement?

...e I had had third ...re, once in 1927 ...beaten up, and I ...ther ones. I'd sign

...nent read to you?"

...s tell you what it

...ever meeting Har... boy, and said he

...go when you were ...o. 5 police station ...s to the detective ...hall."

...there?" "Detec... ...t my face."

... "With his hand," ...to?" "What could ...en he put a state... ...told me to sign ...h rubber hose he

...do?" "I signed." ...se Hose

PADDLE AND THE HOLE ARE CONVICTS' FATES

(Continued from Page One)

trouble. Once a week, each Wednesday, a small ounce packet of tobacco is handed out to each inmate. This is his sole luxury. The packet is known as a "deck of weed."

A Medium of Exchange

All trading, bets, little favors and, in fact, anything that outside would be negotiated through the medium of currency, inside the prison is done on the basis of tobacco. The deck of tobacco, like the dollar, has its fractional purchasing power. Half a deck will have certain well defined values, so will the quarter deck and even the number of "drags" (smokes) to a deck is clearly defined and each has its own definite value.

"Tobacco, the prison medium of trade, was first obtained as a sequence to a former riot and this prison tradition undoubtedly played a part in the recent agitation.

"Tobacco is smoked in the pipe, a prison issue, but by far the greater number of inmates prefer it in cigarette form and deeply resent anything that prevents them so using it. To smoke cigarettes one must have paper as well as tobacco and until quite recently, though cigarette papers are not an issue, a paper was supplied to the men for other purposes that was suitable for cigarette making and largely used as such. Recently, however, through what we outsiders regard as the departmental blunder of some purchasing agent, a paper of another quality was substituted, a thick green paper, akin to blotting paper, impossible for use in cigarette making. This is one active cause of the trouble. The discontent was growing before I came out a few weeks ago and there were signs of trouble ahead. We could all see it coming and I have been told only to-day that the authorities at least suspected the situation for no outside gangs were out the afternoon before and no workers were allowed in the ...

there, and prisoners like separate cells. We lived in a compound with a 16-foot barbed wire fence around it. At night we were locked in dormitories and there was no privacy. There was no educational work there, no language or other classes as at the penitentiary proper, only work at the trades and real hard never-ending labor, but there was the wind and the sunshine and to me that made up for all the rest.

"Just one more thing I would like to say," he concluded, "and that is the unfairness of launching the released prisoner on the world again with nothing but a $10 bill. Released, he craves the society of the other sex, and in two days his money is all gone again and the only people to whom he can turn for help are his former prison associates."

Want to Go Straight

"Can one wonder that he goes back again? Most fellows want to go straight. Some channel of legitimate labor should be provided for them. In this way only in most cases can they gather the means to reestablish themselves in the world again."

A second educated man, also released recently from "K.P." fully endorsed the above. He added something new by way of comment on other angles of the penal institution.

"The cigarette paper was the real cause of the trouble," he endorsed. "It was not the food, the food is good enough, though not luxurious. I was in the penitentiary and not in the preferred prison. In the penitentiary one gets up early, gets cleaned up, gets one's breakfast tray and carries it to one's cell and there eats the meal. Each day we got an exercise period and did our allotted tasks, returning for mid-day and evening meals. We were allowed books to read and the labor was not excessive.

"The aristocracy of the prison were the 'lifers.' They formed their own select rings and we 'short timers' were not admitted to them. The lifer on the principal that 'it is wisest to make the best of a bad job,' organizes his prison life to get the very best out of it. He is there for good and he is extraordinarily resourceful in this regard and being one of the 'select' gets the benefit of the older

inmates of Kingston penitentiary. The Star's informant had some interesting things to say of men who in the past have figured much in the public eye.

Some Familiar Names

"Gordon Simpson, 'Red' Ryan's old pal, and companion of some of his escapades, is working now in the kitchen as chief butcher," he said. "Despite the prison fare he is still a Hercules in strength. He spends his spare time in reading good books and is a model prisoner. Bill Murrell, a convicted murderer, whose sentence was commuted to life imprisonment, is working hard in the stone shacks, where he has become an expert stone-cutter.

"'Shorty' Bryans, another partner of 'Red' Ryan's, is now a yardman inside the prison. He trims the grass, cleans up the snow, and levels the road there. Another interesting character I met was Randall Robinson, the stick-up man who was sentenced to fifteen years, got a parole, turned evangelist, and then received a sentence of another ten years for suborination of perjury.

"'Two-gun O'Brien,' sentenced to fifteen years, is a very much changed man to-day. I saw him down there. He was a regular wreck. When he went down to Kingston he reckoned he was going to revolutionize the institution. Placed in the blacksmith's shop because he was a machinist, with two other men he tried to make a gun. He got caught, and did six months in the hole in addition to get frequent paddling.

"'Doris Macdonald, involved in a murder on the Lachine Rd. and sentenced to life, is still down there. She was recently operated on for appendicitis. She may get out before her time is up, as I understand someone has promised to marry her and give her a new start in life.

A Penitentiary Hymn Writer

"Then there is William Swimmings, Salvation Army man from Ottawa, sentenced for an assault. He spends his time writing hymns and in constant prayer. He is unpopular with the other men because he sometimes makes disturbances in his fervor.

taken out of the line and placed in the dungeon.

Word of the imprisonment of the "innocent" spread rapidly through the penitentiary. The convicts refused to work in the afternoon.

"Take him out of the Hole, take him out of the Hole—take him out of the Hole," was the cry raised regularly by the inmates. This demand was kept up during the day and far into the night.

Friday the inmates were allowed out of their cells and no one was done at the penitentiary.

The Star's informant states there had been numerous complaints over the treatment accorded inmates by the guards. Only 25 minutes was allowed each day for exercise purposes in the penitentiary yards and reading material was not allowed in the cells. There had been frequent complaints about the food being wormy.

COATSWORTH FAVORS 'RED' RYAN'S RELEASE

Unofficial Sources Indicate Judge Believes Former Robber Should Get Liberty

Special to The Star

Ottawa, Oct. 20.—It is learned through sources close to those of justice, that Judge Emerson Coatsworth of Toronto, who made a report to the remission branch department of justice on the conviction of Norman James "Red" bank robber, now serving his sentence in Portsmouth penitentiary, that the judge is favorable to his being granted his freedom on ticket-of-leave.

It was Judge Coatsworth, county judge, who sentenced Ryan to life imprisonment.

Ryan pleaded guilty to the charge of holding up and robbing the ...

CHAPTER 7

RED 3

7

*It must all be considered as though spoken by
a character in a novel.*

—Roland Barthes

Hemingway/Callaghan 2

Morley Callaghan wrote about Red Ryan much later
than Ernest Hemingway did. And he didn't write a
bunch of newspaper stories, he wrote a novel called *More Joy
in Heaven.*

The title comes from Luke, chapter 15, in which Jesus
answers the disapproval of those who criticize him for eating
with sinners. In response, he presents them with several par-
ables, including the parable of the lost sheep. He tells them
that a man with a hundred sheep who loses one will leave
the other ninety-nine unattended to search for the one that
is missing. And when he finds it, he will call his friends and
neighbours together to rejoice with him, saying, "I have found

my lost sheep." In the same way, Christ says, there will be more joy in heaven over one sinner repenting than over ninety-nine righteous people who don't need to repent.

In Kingston, a sinner was about to repent.

The Good Thief

The Good Thief was the nickname given by the *Star*'s Roy Greenaway to the Roman Catholic chaplain of Kingston Penitentiary, Father Wilfred Kingsley. The name came from the parish he also served, the Church of the Good Thief, and Greenaway used it liberally throughout a profile of the priest he wrote for the *Star Weekly* in May 1933. It was in that profile that Greenaway introduced Toronto readers to the remarkable influence Kingsley was having on the Golden Boy of Crime.

Greenaway wrote that, upon his return to Kingston, Ryan had been an incorrigible terror to the prison authorities, spending months on end down in the hole. "But his bravado wilted before the eyes and words of the Good Thief."

This wasn't the first readers had heard about the reformation of Red Ryan. A year earlier, in January 1932, a judge in a Toronto courtroom rebuked a lawyer for referring to Ryan as a hardened criminal by saying he "had heard that 'Red' Ryan has become a very estimable citizen." Those comments gave Ryan's childhood friend, *Star* reporter Athol Gow, a hook on which to hang a page-one story in which friends and former inmates testified to the fact that Ryan was "a man completely reformed."

Star readers learned that Ryan's dream now was to open up "a little shop—a cigar store or a haberdashery—in Kingston, not far from the penitentiary." "I'd like to be close enough to the prison so that all my friends, the guards and the officials of the warden's office, could come and visit me regularly," he said.

Readers were told of Ryan's work as a hospital orderly in the prison, and how every spare hour was spent pouring over history books, "his brow wrinkled with wonder as he reads the material he missed during his school days." One ex-inmate friend told of the lectures Ryan regularly gave Kingston's "hardened criminals." They "never heard such lectures as Red gives them. He talks to them like a Dutch uncle. And they are all afraid of him. The whole truth is that Red Ryan is the greatest influence for good now at Kingston penitentiary."

Most importantly, the article gave the first hint that something unthinkable was perhaps being contemplated. It told the story of a prison visit by the federal minister of justice, Ernest Lapointe, who was introduced by the warden to "the notorious 'Red' Ryan."

"You've been here since 1921, haven't you," the minister said.

"Yes, and I guess I'll be here for the rest of my life," Red is said to have replied.

"I wouldn't say that," Mr. Lapointe said. "Things aren't always as bad as they are painted." Then he added: "You don't look like the man I had pictured as the man who held banks in terror."

A combination of interests was beginning to come together—the *Star*'s, Ryan's and the publicity-seeking Father Kingsley's—and a compelling story was starting to be spun.

The story went like this: After wilting Ryan's bravado in the hole, Kingsley elevated Red, both literally and figuratively. First by re-establishing his connection to his Catholic faith, then by deepening his involvement in that faith, asking Ryan to be his sacristan, the person responsible for the sacred vessels and vestments of the church, and finally by bringing Ryan into the hospital to work as an orderly. Throughout all this, Ryan was the reluctant, modest acolyte: unworthy of these gifts and then, after accepting them, devoted to the man who believed in him so strongly.

As Ryan wrote to his brother in a letter that was clearly intended for a wide readership, "I would rather do anything than break the trust placed in me by my kind chaplain, Father Kingsley."

Kingsley, the story went, saw something in Red Ryan that no one else had ever seen: goodness. Ryan, for his part, was determined to prove the priest right. He began writing the story of his life, which he titled "The Futility of Crime," and built little crucifixes inside lightbulbs, which, apparently, didn't seem weird back then.

The real story was slightly less inspirational. Kingsley, whom Ryan's biographer Peter McSherry describes as a "domineering, little pedant" with a mission to "inflict his ideas on the world around him," saw in Ryan a publicity magnet and the perfect vehicle to spread his ideas about prison reform and acquire the prestige he felt entitled to. Ryan saw in Kingsley a path, first of all, to the plum prison job of hospital orderly, which allowed him to move out of the cell blocks and into a nice little room in the hospital, and then, as his story began getting more and more ink, straight out the prison gates.

Greenaway's hagiographic article about the father in the *Star Weekly* appears to have been an exercise in tactics, rather than journalism. The *Star* knew Ryan sold papers. Kingsley was Ryan's gatekeeper. Kingsley had an ego that needed stroking. The *Star* stroked.

Greenaway and Kingsley first hooked up when the reporter was sent to Kingston in October 1932 to cover a series of violent prisoner riots. As Kingsley was making his way through a group of reporters, refusing to answer questions, Greenaway had the bright idea of asking the priest if Ryan had played any part in the rioting. Kingsley took him aside and told the reporter to call on him at midnight.

That was the beginning of a three-year relationship described by Greenaway as filled with long talks, sitting and smoking in Kingsley's office and long drives around the countryside near Kingston. They were working each other: Kingsley to get his name and ideas about penal reform into print, and to ensure the full credit for Ryan's reformation was his; Greenaway to make sure that when Ryan finally did walk out of the gates of Kingston, he would walk—exclusively—towards the reporters from the *Star*. And they both got what they wanted, God help us all.

A Brief Word on the Epigraph

The Barthes quote that opens this chapter probably needs a word or two of clarification, not to explain what it means, but to explain how it got there.

It does look perfect up there, doesn't it? And for the reader, I hope, it leads to all kinds of interesting thoughts. Thoughts like "Yes, that sums it up so well." And "See, that's why I'll never be an author, because I don't possess the kind of literary recall you need to open chapters with perfectly selected quotations." Those are the things I hope you are thinking.

Here's what happened. Feeling deeply procrastinative one day, I wondered if I might distract myself from the task I wasn't doing by filling some pages writing about not writing this book. So I consulted the best book I've ever read on the subject of not writing, *Out of Sheer Rage* by Geoff Dyer, a book about not writing a book about D.H. Lawrence. Fully embracing the ethos of not getting down to work, Dyer opens his book with three quotations, a Lawrence (naturally), a Flaubert and the Barthes I stole.

It is extremely comforting, when you are avoiding writing yourself, to read someone who writes as well as Dyer does go on at considerable length about his avoidance of writing. Of course, that comfort lasts only until you are forced to acknowledge that, while you and Dyer have very similar thoughts on the subject and would probably get along great if you ever met at a prestigious book festival or awards dinner, he is writing his thoughts down—actually working, in other words—whereas you are just reading, which, unfair as that may be, is not really the same thing.

You might try to convince yourself that you are the purist, the true Dyerian, while Dyer is only a poser when it comes to not working, but that kind of thinking can keep you going for only another couple of hours.

Eventually, inevitably, you begin to hate Dyer. You hate his ability to fill page after page with his tiresome humorous riffing and decide you'll very cleverly plagiarize him. Then you decide to get his phone number and make threatening calls. Finally, you take his Barthes quote and put his book back on the shelf.

The Kingston Riots

The riots that brought Greenaway to Kingston worked to Ryan's benefit in two ways: they brought his name back into the public spotlight, and they focused public attention on the need for penal reform. But the riots themselves weren't really much, as prison riots go. Of course, that's easy to say when you're not holed up in a locked cell with a bunch of thieves and murderers running around.

The early reports, as usual, got it wrong. Tim Buck, the leader of the Communist Party of Canada, had been installed in Kingston the year before on a charge of communist agitation. So, predictably, the first reports were full of fears that a communist uprising was taking place. One early report quoted a prison guard saying, "The fact that there were Communist prisoners there naturally would make many people jump at once to the conclusion that the trouble was fomented by Red Russia." Naturally.

It turned out the riots grew out of assorted beefs the

inmates had: brutality on the part of some guards, favouritism and, above all, "the question of cigarette papers," as a *Star* report put it. Apparently the men were not getting enough rolling papers with their tobacco and were using toilet paper to roll their smokes, resulting in many of them developing "cigarette throat."

Red Ryan's name appeared in the riot coverage from the very beginning. The first wave of *Star* coverage included a small "Special" with the headline DENY "RED" RYAN WAS RINGLEADER. It began, "Rumors that Red Ryan had been one of the ringleaders in the mutiny at the penitentiary were denied to-day by one of the guards."

One day later, Red Ryan's status was upgraded to hero, no doubt after a quiet word passed between Kingsley and Greenaway.

It is reported that in the outbreak at the penitentiary Monday, when 500 convicts started a riot in the industrial shops, Ryan came over from the hospital, where he is an orderly, and appealed to the men to return to their work and "play" the game. It is said his appeal was a striking one and helped considerably to restore order.

The fact that this report was pure bunk and denied almost instantly by almost everyone didn't matter. Red Ryan was now the hero of the prison riots and, as the *Star* also reported, he was applying for his ticket-of-leave.

Ticket-of-leave was an early sort of parole at a time when a life sentence meant exactly that. It involved the prisoner making a direct application to the minister of justice. According to the *Star*, the judge who had sentenced Ryan after his capture in Minneapolis supported Ryan's request. The *Star* also felt the need to throw this in:

> Ryan is well liked in Kingston prison. A fine, handsome, clean-cut man, he stands out as a giant among the inmates.

A short burst of pro–Red Ryan stories popped up in the *Star*, with headlines like "RED" RYAN'S NEW CHARACTER SEEN IN GRATEFUL LETTER and WOULD SET "RED" RYAN FREE AS LECTURER TO WILD LADS. But despite the *Star*'s best efforts, the justice minister refused to issue Ryan's ticket-of-leave.

Dr. Oswald Withrow

But here the second effect of the Kingston riots started working in Ryan's favour. The nation's prison system was going through a crisis. The Kingston riots were just the first of about a dozen across the country over the next three years. Prison reform was being demanded not just by rioting inmates, but by opposition politicians and the press. Caught up in the spirit of the moment, the *Globe* decided it wanted a piece of the Red Ryan story too. And for that, it turned to Dr. Oswald C.J. Withrow.

Oswald Withrow had been sent to Kingston in 1927, convicted of manslaughter after a twenty-one-year-old woman
died following an abortion he performed. He spent two and
a half years there, working with Ryan in the prison hospital.
They became friends, reportedly spending Sundays together
talking about history and philosophy and prison reform. Upon
his release, prison reform became Withrow's burning cause.

He wrote a series of articles for the *Globe* on the issue and,
in his front-page article of August 28, 1933, he enlisted Ryan
in the fight. Here's how the editors set the piece up:

```
Today Dr. Withrow introduces Globe
readers to a new "Red" Ryan. The
young bank bandit of yesteryear, he
tells us, has "turned a new leaf" and
become a new man.
```

And here's how Withrow begins:

```
"What is 'RED' RYAN actually like?"
    Scores have asked me that ques-
tion. You too, are expecting an
answer. This, then, is the real
"Red" Ryan as I came to know him
by daily contact through our work in
the Hospital. It's hard to write this
character sketch. For "Red" is my
friend. I like him. I believe in him.
And the press has always presented
```

```
him, in glaring headlines and yel-
lowed columns, as one of the worst
men in the whole world.
```

"Yellowed" would be clear to readers in 1933 as meaning "yellow journalism," the use of crude exaggeration and sensationalism, rather than facts, to sell papers. The antithesis, in other words, of what Withrow and the *Globe* were up to.

```
This man ... is really scrupulously
clean in mind and body. I have not
heard him use profane language....
He does not use tobacco in any form.
He is tall, muscular and strong. He
has a clear and steady eye. He keeps
himself fit by daily physical training
in his cell and by a brisk walk of
many miles each day on the triangular
gravel path of ninety paces in front
of the hospital. Yet he is as tender
as any female nurse in his treatment
of the sick men confided to his care.
```

Kind of a cross between Lou Gehrig and Florence Nightingale, although Withrow had a different model in mind.

```
I am reminded of the description
of David of sacred history, "Now
he was ruddy withal of a beautiful
```

> countenance and goodly to look to."
> This is "Red" Ryan in the flesh.

So there.

The article also includes perhaps the most ridiculous excuse for Ryan's life of crime of them all. According to Withrow, at fifteen years of age, Ryan and his delinquent pals decided they were through with crime after spending a few weeks in jail on remand. When they arrived at Police Court, the Crown attorney asked them what their plans were.

> Boyishly and tremblingly they replied
> that they had made up their minds
> to go straight. "What do they say?"
> questioned the Magistrate. "They say,
> your Worship, that they will continue
> to live lives of crime." "Very well,
> then, five years in the penitentiary."

So it was all the fault of an evil Crown attorney and a deaf judge who, in the movie, will be holding one of those metal listening horns to his ear when he asks his question.

To his larger point, Withrow makes it clear that Ryan's prison transformation was the work of the ex-bank robber and his saintly priest, Father Kingsley, alone. The fact that it happened in Kingston Penitentiary, in a broken penal system badly in need of reform, could almost be considered a miracle.

I desire to make it perfectly clear
that the System had nothing whatever to do with this genuine reformation. Had the System had its way
"Red" would now be a broken bit of
humanity, still under forty years of
age. But there was something in this
friend of mine, superior to his surroundings, which caused him to lay
hold of a higher ideal of life and
cling to it through these many years.

Ryan's reformation happened despite the system, and despite
that reformation, the system still held him in its clutches.

Unless his exceptional record inter-
cedes for him and the System becomes
more human and considerate he must
stay on in the Big House.

The article was a brilliant public case for prison reform.
And a textbook PR campaign. It featured a celebrity, which
was guaranteed click-bait long before there was such a
thing as clicks. And not just any celebrity—Red Ryan, the
dashing bank robber and famous rogue who had charmed
a nation by foiling authorities on both sides of the border
while stealing hundreds of thousands of dollars. Now, with
the help of a sainted priest, the former bad boy had reformed
and was fighting, alone and against all odds, for the benefit

of his fellow inmates, inmates trapped in a cruel, medieval prison system based on punishment and on the impossibility of reform. But isn't Ryan himself a living, breathing, David-like demonstration that reform is possible for even the worst offenders? The case never seemed so solid. A letter to the editor of the *Globe*, shortly after Withrow's article about Ryan appeared, demonstrates just how extensive the support for the reformers was.

> To the Editor of The Globe: I have been following with great interest the articles of Dr. Withrow regarding conditions in Kingston Penitentiary, and as an ex-member of the Criminal Investigation Branch of the R.C.M.P., who after the escape of Norman ("Red") Ryan in 1923 was for some four months employed on an investigation at the institution, I would most certainly say that an investigation of conditions and of the entire penal system of the country is long overdue.

Even the guys in the white hats were onside.

Obviously, none of this hurt Red Ryan's cause either. By December 1934, both the *Globe* and the *Star* confidently predicted in front-page stories that Red Ryan would be freed from prison early in the new year. The *Globe*'s story, based on "reliable information," said that, upon his release, Ryan would work as Father Kingsley's gardener at the Church of the Good Thief. The *Star* also said Ryan would work as Kingsley's gardener, but had the rare sense to refer to the news as a "rumour." The next day's *Star* confirmed that rumour by claiming the paper had received confirmation from the prime minister's office. His freedom would be a "yule present," the *Star* confidently claimed.

When the *Star* had to backtrack a week later, it floated two theories for the communication mix-up. One supposed that, it being winter, "gardening activities are now at a very low ebb in Kingston." It was also possible, the *Star* said, that a promise of parole "at the end of *a* year" had been misheard as "at the end of *the* year." In any case, Red Ryan celebrated Christmas behind bars.

A small item in the May 8, 1935, *Globe* sounds almost forlorn. "About twenty-five more convicts were released from Kingston Penitentiary today in connection with the King's Silver Jubilee amnesty. . . . It was learned definitely 'Red' Ryan was not one of those released." There's something almost passive-aggressive in the use of the word "more."

One ingredient was still missing before the final scene in this redemption story could play out. Releasing Red Ryan from prison would require a bold political act, and bold political acts are almost always acts of desperation. Luckily for Red Ryan, an unpopular government was about to head to the polls.

Richard Bedford Bennett

There is no statue of R.B. Bennett on Parliament Hill in Ottawa. Canada's eleventh prime minister left behind an impressive list of achievements during his five years in office. He was responsible for instituting unemployment insurance and the minimum wage. He created the Bank of Canada and the broadcasting commission that would become the CBC.

But that's not what he's remembered for. Bennett's time in office coincided almost exactly with the very worst years of the Great Depression, and his legacy is subsumed in images from those years. Bennett buggies were automobiles with the engines removed, pulled by teams of horses, because the owners couldn't afford gas. Bennett blankets were the newspapers homeless people covered themselves with to keep warm at night.

He was a remarkable man. Born poor, he made himself into probably the richest prime minister in Canadian history. First a teacher, and then a lawyer and extremely shrewd investor, he served in municipal, territorial and provincial governments before heading to Ottawa as a member of Parliament. He won elections and lost elections and finally, at the age of sixty, achieved his goal of becoming prime minister in 1930. His timing in business was perfect. His timing in politics sucked.

Personally, he was a bit of a dandy, but an odd one. According to his biographer, John Boyko, he decided in his early twenties that he would present a more impressive appearance if he weren't so thin, so he began eating three huge, fatty meals every day and a pound of chocolate every night before bed and avoided all exercise except for a short walk every Sunday afternoon. Amazingly, he survived well into his seventies. He wore bowler hats long after they had gone out of fashion and even his walking-around suit jackets were cut

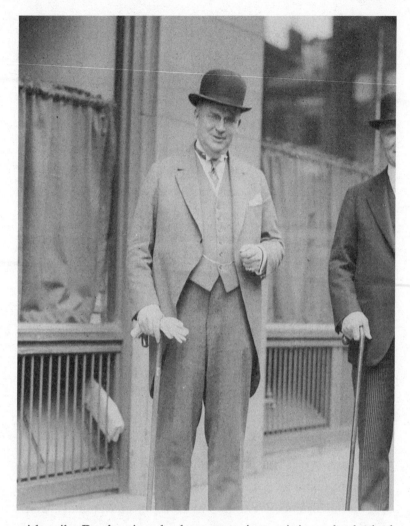

with tails. By the time he became prime minister, he looked like a cross between the Lionel Barrymore character from *It's a Wonderful Life* and the Monopoly mascot, which was not the best look to be sporting when the country was starving and out of work.

He never drank but could talk knowledgably about wine for hours. He was incredibly generous. Throughout his life he made tremendously large donations to schools (over $1 million to Dalhousie University alone) and other charitable causes. All through the Depression, as prime minister, he would receive letters from Canadians seeking assistance. In hundreds of cases, those letters were answered with a personal note and a five-dollar bill from his own pocket.

A lifelong bachelor, Bennett had an incredible capacity for work and almost no capacity for delegation. When he was prime minister, he also took on the portfolios of finance and foreign affairs. One newspaper cartoon of the day showed a cabinet room in which every minister sitting at the table was Bennett, all the assistants were Bennett, and every portrait on the wall was a portrait of Bennett.

He was renowned as a brilliant debater and litigator and, almost always, was the smartest man in the room.

Unfortunately, for all his gifts, he wasn't equipped to handle the great hardships of the Depression. In 1932, his government passed one of the most unpopular laws in Canadian history, the Relief Act. Under the terms of the act, work camps were set up in remote locations for unemployed single men with no job prospects. Camp conditions were terrible, the work was brutal, and the subsistence-level pay was 20 cents a day, plus 1.3 cents a day for cigarettes. To protest conditions in the camps, thousands of camp workers mobilized in the west and started riding the rails to Ottawa, picking up more protesters along the way. It was called the On to Ottawa trek, but the trekkers didn't make it that far. In Regina, Bennett ordered the RCMP to attack the men and jail the protest leaders. In the riot that ensued, one cop died and hundreds of workers were injured.

In 1935, facing re-election and the full-on hatred of the country, he broadcast a series of radio speeches modelled on Franklin D. Roosevelt's fireside chats. The content of the speeches owed more than a little to Roosevelt as well. It was Bennett's version of the New Deal, promising more social reforms, more government intervention and an end to *laissez-faire*.

And just in case those sweeping economic measures weren't enough to turn Canadian sentiment back towards Bennett's Tories, he asked for a report on Red Ryan's suitability for a ticket-of-leave.

Prime Minister Bennett had visited Ryan at Kingston Penitentiary the year before. He was in Kingston on other business and had been persuaded by a member of his caucus who had taken up Ryan's cause, a rich Manitoba rancher and senator named H.A. Mullins, to stop by the prison and see Red during his trip. Here's how Red described the encounter in the *Star*:

> I hadn't the slightest warning that I was about to meet the prime minister and I got the shock of my life when I turned and saw him coming toward me. . . .
>
> Mr. Bennett shook hands with me . . . I was so taken aback that I scarcely knew what to say. The premier must have known just how I felt for he was off-hand and friendly and put me at ease.

"Well Ryan," he said as he shook
hands, "I've heard quite a bit about
you." I said, "I've heard quite a
bit about you, sir, and read quite a
bit too." This seemed to tickle Mr.
Bennett and he laughed heartily.

Apparently, after a forty-five-minute conversation, Bennett
asked to see Ryan's cell, where, again apparently, he was
impressed by its neatness and by the quality of the books Ryan
was reading. No promises were made, but you'd think, at the
very least, Ryan would feel encouraged about his prospects for
freedom after a personal visit from the leader of the country.

Bennett was a smart guy, so I don't know what he made
of Ryan. Certainly there were political reasons to set him free.
A thankful Red Ryan would be singing the prime minister's
praises on the front pages of the newspapers for several days.
Also, as a rebuke to the opposition's calls for massive prison
reform, how bad could Canada's prisons be if even the notorious Red Ryan was reformed in one of them? The prime minister's personal secretary told Peter McSherry many years later
that Bennett's "strong element of personal kindness" may have
been responsible for his involvement. In any event, and despite
the fact that Ryan's suitability report did not recommend his
release, Prime Minister Bennett did something that had never
been done before. He gave Ryan a one-day leave to attend the
funeral of his sister.

Ryan spent July 2, 1935, in Toronto. The funeral was early
in the morning, and he passed the rest of the day visiting

relatives and touring a city that had changed quite a bit since he'd last seen it in 1924. The *Star*, of course, tagged along for the ride.

> He visited High Park and the pink
> colored flamingos from Cuba, in the
> bird sanctuary, caught his eye. So
> did the new electric flashing colored
> signs at Sunnyside. The Star build-
> ing and the Bank of Commerce building
> also aroused his curiosity.

Readers also learned that Ryan stopped by a movie theatre briefly "to hear for a few seconds a real 'talkie' for the first time in his life."

The young prison guard who spent that day watching Ryan told Peter McSherry more than forty-five years later that his prisoner seemed to be addicted to publicity. Despite the concern expressed by members of his family that too much press might hurt his chances of parole, Ryan couldn't get enough. "You couldn't tell Ryan that this publicity could hurt him," the guard said. "He wouldn't listen. He wanted the attention. He had to have it."

And he was more than happy to say the right things about the prime minister:

> "I am going to write Premier Bennett and thank him for his courtesy and kindness to me. He has a big heart. He has kept faith with me."

Timing

Ryan had one other thing going for him, which should be mentioned briefly. There may have never been a time in history as kind to bank robbers as the 1930s.

With so many people thrown out of their houses and off their farms by the banks, bank robbers, such as Bonnie and Clyde and Pretty Boy Floyd, were folk heroes. It's not an exaggeration to say that when good people were reading in their newspapers about the exploits of the G-men tracking down John Dillinger, they were pulling for Dillinger.

A popular joke at the time concerned a banker getting a young farmer's daughter pregnant. When the banker offered to marry the girl, her father said no. He'd sooner have a bastard in the family than a banker.

So the Ace of Canadian Bank Robbers (ret'd) probably enjoyed even more support, just based on the popularity of his former career.

Freedom

Everyone now seemed to agree that it was no longer a question of if Ryan would be released, merely when.

"When" came three weeks later.

On July 23, 1935, the warden of Kingston Penitentiary passed on the news to his star inmate. Red Ryan was a free man.

"Prison reformers rejoiced," wrote Roy Greenaway, thirty years later, "and henceforth Ryan was to be an example for the whole world."

If you've already checked out the horizontal shot of our boy in Chapter 14, you have a pretty good idea of how that went.

By the way, Bennett lost the election three months after Ryan was released. In fact, he got creamed.

CHAPTER
8

WHY HISTORY?

8

I heard a historian being interviewed recently. He was asked why he had decided to make history his life's work. He replied, "History allows us to see where we are."

So let's take a look.

This book is history. It's about a headline-craving narcissist with an almost complete lack of morality, whose entire life's journey was propelled by fake news. I guess that does help us to see where we are. Unfortunately it doesn't do much to explain why, after watching this show so many times before, we are we still watching it today.

If recent events have taught us anything, it's that history doesn't move in a straight line. Despite what the old newsreels told us, progress isn't always marching forward. We circle back. We learn, and then we forget what we learned. We tell ourselves, after falling for a particularly seductive line of BS, that we'll never fall for that kind of thing again. And then the next scam artist appears, and we fall even harder. Or, more and more, we refuse to even acknowledge we've been had. We ignore evidence although it stares us in the face. We pretend it isn't there and double down on the idiocy. We spit in the face of truth.

How can history teach anything to people who refuse to see reality? It can't. What history can do is chronicle the particulars of our blind spots and failings in the hope that, if we somehow manage to come up with a way to save this planet, and if the generations that follow ours have a sincere desire to be better than we are, we will have left them a record of what not to do.

Another thing history allows us to do is compare stuff today with stuff from the past. In this case, it allows us to compare the quality of journalism today, which gets a pretty bad rap, to the quality of the journalism of eighty or ninety years ago.

One of the ways we can judge quality is to ask ourselves, Is this object, or tool, or service satisfying in both objective and subjective ways? A Fender Telecaster, for example, sounds great, plays great and is a beautiful object. It is, therefore, a quality instrument. You can say the same about the Jaguar E-type roadsters from the 1960s. They were fast, relatively inexpensive (if your relative was a Ferrari or an Aston Martin) and probably the most beautiful cars ever designed. Quality.

In architecture the same tests apply. The sense of soul-lessness one feels walking—or more likely, driving—through a new suburban development is a reaction to a lack of quality. The designs aren't new or innovative; they are derivative and out of proportion. The materials are cheap and ugly. The layout of the streets promotes isolation and gets in the way of the creation of community. New communities do satisfy many of the objective needs of twenty-first-century North Americans: affordability, ease of commuting, private outdoor space. And they satisfy many more of our wants: large walk-in closets, three-car garages, neighbourhoods full of people who are just like us. But no sane person would ever suggest that the houses we are building in the hundreds of thousands around our cities have any subjective value beyond those narrow considerations. These homes will never be considered objects of beauty. There is no future revival movement to look forward to when the original is a vinyl and stucco pastiche, designed by an algorithm.

Contrast that with the brownstones of New York, or the row houses of St. John's: homes that satisfy us as places to live, places to connect with neighbours, places from which to walk to work or school, and beautiful objects in their own right. I think, in terms of quality, it's safe to say about architecture, "They don't build 'em like they used to."

But can you say the same thing about journalism? I've already written about truth in journalism, but what about quality?

It's easy to look at journalism today and conclude it used to be much better. We remember when newspapers were fat with international, national and local coverage, written and edited with care and competence. We remember when news programs and news networks featured plenty of reporters in the field and aired documentaries that challenged our thinking about ourselves and our place in the world.

But those conversations and that journalism, on all our broadcast media, are largely disappearing now, replaced by the cheap, easy sameness of political panels and personal stories. And newspapers, with very few exceptions, look more like supermarket handouts than the papers of twenty or thirty years ago.

Objectively, daily journalism (and, once again, there are exceptions—some of the major papers have never been better and public radio still manages to do some good things with dwindling resources) is not satisfying our needs. It is not helping us become more informed citizens. In fact, it's beginning to have the opposite effect. Our journalism is splitting us apart and creating factions living with different versions of the truth. It has helped to create, along with politicians and political operatives, the age of alternative facts.

That's the objective take. Subjectively, and this almost goes without saying, journalism is also failing to meet any basic standards. The writing tends to be slapdash and clichéd. The editing is usually poor or non-existent. There is very little style, and certainly almost nothing remotely approaching beauty.

So, we can agree that there is a lack of quality in today's journalism, but is it like architecture? Have we lost our way after centuries of craftsmanship and style? Was it, like architecture, always better before?

I think, when it comes to journalism, it's more the case that a very brief flourishing of the craft—which began with the rise of professionalism in the 1970s and ended with the destruction of the traditional media caused by Facebook and the rest of the social media giants within the past decade—has been confused with a much longer run of quality work. This is particularly true for daily journalism; magazines have been better for much longer.

Daily journalism was always hack work. Back in Red Ryan's day the pay was terrible, the hours were brutal and the boss treated you like crap. A beat reporter today is a rarer bird than back then, which is a shame, and a less flamboyant character, also a shame, but there is more professionalism. While the writing may be flatter and less sensational, today's reporter is also less likely to be in the pocket of someone at city hall, less likely to be lazy with research and quotes, and less likely to spend the mornings hungover and the afternoons drinking.

Personally, I love the journalism from the first half of the twentieth century, and I'm trying my best to emulate that lazy, loose and flamboyant style in this book, but I would never claim that, as journalism, it was quality work. A lot of it was great, sure, but very little was good. You can enjoy reading Hemingway's pieces on the Kingston prison break. You can enjoy his pared-down writing and the way he propels the narrative forward. You can enjoy his novelistic style and the way it contrasts with the standard newspaper reporter's technique. You can even, in hindsight, enjoy it as an example of the early stylistic growth of a great writer. But, for God's sake, don't try to fact-check it. You might as well try to fact-check one of his short stories.

I'm usually not a fan of "golden age" thinking. It tends to be employed mainly by nativist bigots, for one thing. But when it comes to journalism, at least in North America, there is a case to be made that there was a relatively brief golden age, triggered chiefly by the *Washington Post*'s take-down of Richard Nixon. That event inspired the age of the young, crusading reporter, which led to an explosion of journalism schools, which pushed the old, cynical hack reporters of yesteryear to the margins, which took us right up to the internet age and the collapse of the print and broadcast media funding models. The end of the twentieth century was a great time to be a reporter, and a great time to be a news consumer. It isn't a great time for either of those things today. And it probably wasn't back when Canada's Jesse James was on the front page.

Every few years, you will read about a small movement to pressure Ottawa to erect a monument to honour R.B. Bennett on Parliament Hill. An artist in New Brunswick actually has a statue all ready to go. It hasn't happened yet, but Bennett fans can always visit this small plaque-on-a-plinth in a park in downtown Calgary, the city in which he first made his name.

It's a modest tribute. But we are a modest people.

EARNED REST

'RED' RYAN CAPTURED IN REVOLVER DUEL WITH POLICE SQUAD

Hamilton Bank Bandit, Who Escaped From Kingston, Is Wounded and Overpowered in Minneapolis, Where He Was Getting His Mail

Dangerous Criminal Again Behind Bars

THREE CONFEDERATES MANAGE TO ESCAPE

Patrolman and Two Bystanders Shot When Fugitives Are Cornered —Gangsters Narrowly Evaded Capture in Toronto Less Than Month Ago

Canadian Press Despatch

Minneapolis, Dec. 14.—Four escaped convicts, who were surprised after leaving the Minneapolis postoffice tonight, shot and wounded a policeman and two bystanders. One of the gunmen was captured and taken to police headquarters, where he gave the name of "Red" Ryan.

All four of the men are alleged to have escaped from the penitentiary at Kingston, Ont., by setting fire to the prison barn and climbing over the walls. Later they are alleged to have robbed banks at Detroit and Chicago.

Patrolman Seriously Injured.

Those shot were Patrolman Norman L. Schurf, seriously wounded; Gustaf Erickson, Minneapolis, slightly wounded; Carl Erickson, son of Gustaf, slightly wounded.

The four men followed to Minneapolis about a week ago, and were seen to collect mail regularly at the general delivery window. Tonight when they called they were followed by eight patrolmen, detectives and secret service operatives.

Bullet Misses Mark.

When they got to the sidewalk one of the detectives closed in on the quarter. Ryan drew a gun and part of one of the detectives; the bullet missed its mark, and struck Gustaf Erickson.

Then, a moment later, Ryan's companions whipped out their revolvers and started firing as they ran. Police returned the fire, and one of the bullets wounded Ryan in the shoulder.

The bandit ran into the front entrance of a clothing store and

OBREGON IN FIELD; TAKES COMMAND OF 8,000 TROOPS

Intercepts Cavalry Attempting to Join With Estrada

YAQUIS ARE VOLUNTEERING

Special Despatch to The Globe

Monterey, Dec. 14.—The censorship in Mexico City suddenly was lifted at almost midnight last night and Obregonistas along the frontier from frontier swept last night a torrent about the possible suppression of the rebellion now in progress at Puebla and on following.

On the Western front, federal revolutionaries under General E. three Estrada, about 5,000 soldiers under President Obregon, surrounding them the north around Lake Chapala in the direction Guadalajara. In the second city Mexico. The number of the Estradas is not clear, but is estimated at about 8,000.

Was Minor Clash.

The forces clashed yesterday Ocotlan, but the engagement was a minor one. The main body of Estrada seemed to get into positions.

BRITISH IMMIGRANT IS ELLIS ISLE VICTIM

Awaiting Permission to Enter U. S. Woman Dies From Pneumonia

CHILD ALSO SUFFERER

Associated Press Despatch

New York, Dec. 14.—Ben Dodge, an Englishman who was here to welcome to a new home in Boston his wife and baby daughter, Kathleen, passengers on the steamship which arrived Monday from England, today greeted and bade a last farewell to his wife. She died yesterday at Ellis Island, of pneumonia contracted while she awaited permission to enter this country in a

ut Ocean Liners On Montreal Route

Canadian Press Cable

LONDON, Dec. 14. — It is good that the Cunard company is about to make an important new development in Canadian services. One or more of the large ships now be transferred to the New York service, and Montreal services.

Cunard Company announced tonight that the ships in operation were the Coronia and Carmania, and that the service will commence next. The developments mean largely in sailings, amounting to seas to more than two a

CHAPTER
9

FOOTNOTES

9

The deeper I get into this project, the less it resembles a book. Reading it over, it seems to me more like an extended series of riffs. It's almost as if I've been jotting down the footnotes to a written life without actually writing the life itself. I assure you that this wasn't my intent. I wonder how it happened.

The concept is not original. The Spanish novelist Enrique Vila-Matas has written a book entirely composed of footnotes to a non-existing work, although his writer-narrator would dispute that. He would say rather that the text was invisible, that it was being held in a kind of suspension somewhere in the literature of the future. To be clear, that is not a claim I am making about this book.

Vila-Matas's book is called *Bartleby & Co.,* and it's an in-depth examination of what he calls "the literature of the No." It's a compendium of footnotes about non-writers actively engaged in the act of not writing.

One of the footnotes concerns the non-writer Bobi Bazlen, who once said, "I believe it is no longer possible to write books. That is why I no longer write them. Virtually all books are no more than footnotes, inflated until they become volumes. That is why I write only footnotes."

Bazlen never wrote a book, although his friends were convinced he had hidden away a major work to be discovered after his death. They were wrong. Five years after his death, a collection of footnotes taken from his notebooks by, presumably, those same friends was published as *Note senza testo (Notes without a Text).* This is what can happen when you die without destroying your notebooks first. Or when you leave too many friends behind.

Vila-Matas's narrator says the fact Bazlen didn't write formed an essential part of his work. "His very existence," he writes, "seems to signal the true end of literature, of the absence of output, the death of the author." Which is very interesting to me, but doesn't really have a lot to do with what's going on here, with this book.

One section of the Vila-Matas book that does seem to have some application to this work is when he takes up the subject of vanity, which was always the driving force propelling the story of Red Ryan. Not surprisingly, the practitioners of the literature of the No didn't have much time for vanity or fame. Their patron saint, the Swiss author Robert Walser, described himself as "a walking nobody who wished to be forgotten."

"The traces Robert Walser left on his path through life," writes W.G. Sebald, "were so faint as to have been almost effaced altogether." He had no possessions: no house, no furniture, not even the tools he needed to write. Sebald believed Walser didn't even own copies of the books he had written.

The last twenty-eight years of his life were spent in what Vila-Matas's narrator describes as "ambiguous silence." He calls it "a commentary on the vanity of all initiative, the vanity of life itself. Perhaps that is why he only wanted to be a walking nobody."

"Vanity and fame," he concludes, "are ridiculous."

Five years before Walser's self-imposed silence began, a bank robber holed up in Minneapolis came to a different conclusion about worldly possessions. Red Ryan realized that his cash, clothes, cars and cufflinks only had value if his friends knew about them. And so he wrote to tell them.

He basically never stopped writing after that. You can argue about how many of the words were actually his, but his name appeared on two memoirs, the early *"Red" Ryan's Rhymes and Episodes* and the (unpublished) prison memoir, "The Futility of Crime." Excerpts from his many prison letters to family members and political bigwigs were often published in the newspapers. He wrote a series of front-page features for the *Star* after his release from prison in 1935 and, if you believe some, he also wrote and broadcast a weekly radio program, using his own life story to deliver the message that crime does not pay.

He was a happy practitioner of the literature of the Me, who apparently never grew tired of his subject matter and never suffered from writer's block. He was an anti-Walser.

Is it possible that Vila-Matas's book of footnotes can help me explain what's happening with this book? Can it help me figure out why it seems so light and unmoored? Perhaps.

Joseph Joubert is another of his writers of the No. He was born in 1754 and died seventy years later. He never wrote a book but spent his life preparing to write one. It was a life-long search for the right conditions. That he never succeeded in that search didn't trouble him, because of the unexpected joy he encountered in his digressions.

He wrote about the difficulty of his task in his diaries: "But how to look in the right place when one does not even know what one is looking for? This happens whenever one composes and creates. Fortunately, by digressing, one does not simply make a discovery, one has happy encounters."

Happy encounters.

I wonder if, either by inclination, or as a consequence of many years practising the short-form writing required by radio, or simply due to an inability to continue with a train of thought for more than a thousand words, I have, without knowing it, become a disciple of the man described in *Bartleby & Co.* as quite possibly the founder of the art of digression?

I must say I do like the sound of happy encounters. Whether it's appropriate to include them in the story of a bank robber and murderer is another question altogether.

"RED" RYAN REPORT DENIED BY WARDEN

Rumors of Notorious Criminal's Escape
Heard in Toronto

Rumors that the notorious "Red" Ryan had escaped from Kingston Penitentiary and might be on his way from Kingston to Toronto caused considerable agitation among the few persons awake in downtown Toronto early this (Monday) morning. The rumors were quickly spiked, however, when a long-distance call to the Warden of the penitentiary elicited the information that, so far as the Warden was aware, "Red" was still securely locked in his cell. Neither were there any other convicts at liberty to his knowledge, said the Warden. The rumors originated in the neighborhood of the Union Station, where, reports had it, railway police were diligently and thoroughly inspecting all freight trains from the east in expectation of the arrival of Canada's most notorious criminal.

If I were making a movie about Red Ryan, the first scene wouldn't take place for another six years after that *Globe* story ran on March 18, 1929. It would be set on the Kingston railway station platform, with a man waiting for the seven o'clock train to Toronto.

INDEX
...s—14-16 Amusements—11
...ets—12-13 Serial—30-31
...—20 Births, Deaths—25
...rban—10 Want Ads—25-29
...en's—22-24 Comics—30-32

THE TORONTO DAIL[Y]

...RD YEAR JUNE CIRCULATION, 246,143 TORONTO, WEDNESDAY, JULY 24, 1935—34 PAGES

ANGUISH OVER WIFE MARS RY...

...int Judge's Report Favors 'Pen' Inspector

HOME AND SPORT EDITI...

...ED' RYAN, FREE, HEARTSICK TO FIND YOUNG WIFE'S LETTERS OF DEVOTION KEPT FROM HIM FOURTEEN YEARS

...utal,' Says the Priest—Ex-Lifer Heard She Died in 1927

...E COULDN'T REPLY

...aroled to Chaplain's Supervision—Doesn't Have to Report to Police

...he happiest man perhaps in all ...nada for the second time this ...nth—and at the same time per...s the saddest—left Kingston ...itentiary last evening and ...rded the 7.07 p.m. train for ...ronto.

...he man was Norman "Red" ...an, reformed "lifer," in whom ...emier R. B. Bennett, Rev. W. T. ...ngsley, Roman Catholic prison ...aplain, prison guards and a host ...other people have pinned their ...th that he will "go straight."

...he unprecedented leave that was ...nted to him to attend his sister's ...neral on July 3 was repeated in ...en more striking fashion yester...y in his ticket of leave papers. ...r the first time in the history of ...nadian penitentiaries, illustrative ... the surety the authorities feel ...out his thorough reform, a ...soner does not have to report to ...lice authorities. Ryan has been ...aced directly under the super...ion of Father Kingsley, to whom ...ust go the credit for the change ... the man. In large typewritten ...d capital letters underlined in red ... the bottom of "Red's" ticket of ...ave are the words: "Upon the ex...ress additional condition that he ...ccept the supervision of the Rev. ...T. Kingsley."

Temporarily released on July 3, ...yan attended the funeral service ...f his favorite, invalid sister whom ...e had hoped to see before she died. ...free man last night, the handwriting of a woman in letters un...elivered for fourteen years tight...ned a band of sudden grief around ...is heart.

Tells Her Devotion

These were the letters from his young wife that Ryan had longed for, but never came. Not even his chaplain had any knowledge of them. For fourteen years, with her picture that she sent him, they had ...een held back from Ryan by un...explainable prison regulations. With a heap of other letters, for all ...hose fourteen years, they remained hidden away in a cupboard of the warden's office.

Sitting beside Father Kingsley in the living room of his devoted ...rother's home last night, Ryan un...folded these missives of a woman who still had faith in him and knowledge of whose devotion would have made a great deal of difference. The famous chaplain, in retreat at St. Augustine's seminary on the Kingston Road with his archbishop and his fellow-members of the Kingston diocese, had driven the nine miles into the city to be one of the first to congratulate Ryan.

Together in hushed silence they glanced at them. They were dated 1921. The handwriting and com...

Leaves Kingston On Side Of Society, Says Ryan

Kingston penitentiary's "Public Exhibit No. 1," as he called himself, the man with a sentence of life and twenty-five years, walked out of the prison gates yesterday virtually a free man.

Whatever emotion he felt, Norman "Red" Ryan hid it behind a cheery smile. He was a perfect example of the advice he gave to many another prisoner: "Keep your chin up."

Thirteen and a half years within the white limestone walls of the grim "Big House" is a long time. Ryan waved them farewell with a gesture of his hand. After all, life is still sweet at 42. Over six feet tall, broad-shouldered, blond, with blue eyes, he set his face toward the new world in which he intends to prove that he has "retired from the banking business for good," as he expressed it.

"I was the true author of my own troubles," was the statement made to-day by the man who in 1923 led the most spectacular break in the history of Canadian penitentiaries and who was rounded up some months later in Minneapolis.

These were almost the same words he used after listening in January, 1924, to the sentence of Judge Coatsworth in Toronto, "imprisonment for life and thirty strokes of the strap." Only seven of these were ever inflicted.

Holds No Animosity

"I never held any animosity toward Judge Coatsworth," Ryan said to-day, as he sat in the study of the Church of the Good Thief, and chatted with Father W. T. Kingsley, the Roman Catholic prison chaplain, the man who, one day years ago stood and looked at Ryan through the bars of the punishment "hole" with understanding, and, gradually, ac-

(Continued on Page 3, Col. 6)

"LUCKY ME! I'M GOING TO CAMP!"

You ought to hear the shouts of excitement when the "Fresh Air Man" visits the heat-swept areas where the poor live and says to Bill or Jim: "It's all fixed; you're going to camp." Dreams have come true. Long weeks of waiting haven't been in vain. The child's ambition to swim in a clear swimming pool, to play in an open field, to see cows and horses—they will all be realized. See the rapture in this boy's face. His happiness can belong to thousands more children who are eagerly, hopefully waiting for the word from The Star Fresh Air Fund, 80 King St. W., that they can go to the country. Make their dream come true!

FURTHE... ARE I... IN LA...

Premier H... ceived Th... sonal C...

McCARD...

Man Belie... Finger A... Can...

Believed ... Labatt kid... blackmail r... threats agai... life, two me... in the St. Th... probably b... next few d... to-day at Q...

Premier H... sonal charge... hunt in an ... those involv... the wealthy ... ago.

Already ... Kingston ... Pete" Murr... London an... alleged to ... Abe", who s... is reported ... Point, Ind., ... police offic... resulted fr...

(Continu...

CONSERVATIVE MORALE ZERO AFTER P.E.I. ANNIHILATION

Even Admit Stevens May Form Official Opposition to Liberals

PREMIER ABSENT

By ROBERT LIPSETT

Ottawa, Ont., July 24.—With the mercury in the 80's and the humidity in the 90's the morale of Bennett Conservatives fell to zero last night as election returns from Prince Edward Island announced complete annihilation of the party in the provincial House.

To-day, for the first time, party stalwarts admitted a clear possibility that Hon. H. H. Stevens will return from the federal elections with the second largest group in the House and in a position to form the official opposition.

Until yesterday's Prince Edward

(Continued on Page 2, Col. 6)

TAKE VACATION AWAY FROM HOME

Mr. and Mrs. Toronto and all the little Torontos are vacationing on a big scale this year. City workers are realizing more than ever the necessity for a complete change and a rest during the annual vacation. Week-ends, too, are being spent out of town to a greater extent.

The planning for both is done through the "Summer Resorts" columns of Star Want Ads., Ontario's best holiday guide. R.S.N., who had a cottage at Moon Lake to rent, and advertised it under this heading, reports numerous calls, so do G.K.Q., who accommodates vacationists on the shore of Lake Simcoe. Mrs. E. S., who rented a cottage at Haliburton, and many, many others. Telephone WA. 3636 to advertise.

MACPHAIL PROBE EXPECTED TO FAVOR 'PEN' INSPECTOR

Understood Judge Daly Is Reluctant to Accept Ex-Convict's Word

GUTHRIE'S REPORT?

By ROBERT LIPSETT

Ottawa, July 24.—Judge E. J. Daly, who sat as a royal commission to investigate charges that Inspector Dawson of the penitentiary staff told Kingston prisoners that Agnes Macphail, M.P., "Made a d—— fool of herself," handed his report to the minister of justice, Hon. Hugh Guthrie, just before noon to-day.

"The report will go before the cabinet and to the governor-general before it is made public," Mr. Guthrie said. "I haven't even read it."

It is understood Judge Daly was reluctant to accept the evidence of an ex-convict against that of a reputable official of the government, and ...

FORESEE GARDINER IN FEDERAL ARENA

By ROBERT LIPSETT

Ottawa, Ont., July 24.—It is believed that within the last 48 hours Premier Gardiner of Saskatchewan has accepted an invitation from Rt. Hon. W. L. Mackenzie King to enter federal politics. If the Liberal party is successful in the next elections, Mr. Gardiner will probably enter the government.

Efforts to have Hon. Chas. Dunning, former minister of finance and of railways, and Mr. Gardiner's predecessor as premier of Saskatchewan, return to the political arena have so far proved fruitless. Friends say Mr. Dunning requires another couple of years to put his personal affairs in order before resuming political life, to which he has already devoted more than twenty years.

indiscreet as to use the terms alleged about a member of parliament ...

SINCLAIR JOINS EXPEDITION SEARCHING MISSING LINK

But Party Is Merely Kashmiri Joyride for Wandering Scribe

STONE ONLY FIND

By GORDON SINCLAIR

Upper Kashmir.—If anyone had told me a year ago that I might one day hunt for the missing link I'd have told them they were just plain balmy.

But to-day, as an outsider who happened to have time on his hands and curiosity in his head, I joined the Yale-Cambridge North India expedition and prowled across the rooftop of the world in search of the first man who ever walked this earth.

In doing so I was pinch-hitting for one of the greatest but least known skeleton hunters to ever dig up a jaw. He, oddly enough, was a Toronto man, the late Dr. Davidson Black.

Although the oldest authentic skeleton of a man—the Neanderthal

(Continued on Page 8, Col. 2)

STAR FRESH AIR FUND

Amount previously acknowledged	$11,540.23
A Grimsby Friend, Mrs. J. N.	5.00
Proceeds of a bazaar held by Eleanor Barless, Helen Brenton and Aileen Pryor	6.66
Jean MacInnes	1.00
Two Friends, E. K. N. and H. W.	2.00
Collected by some children under the name of "Acton Kazoo Band," Jeanne and Sammy Brunelle, Warren Wood and Charlie Rushmere of Acton	5.31
Elizabeth Wyatt, Cannington	2.00
In loving memory of Mr. Isaiah Winters, Collingwood, Ont.; he loved the kiddies	3.60
Proceeds of a sale of lemonade held by Joan Davis, Anne Chisholm, Joan Keen and Charlotte O'Grady, Oakville, Ont.	1.85
Donation by the Liberal Picnic held at Fairmount Park on July 20th	11.48
Proceeds of a bazaar held by Roma Ellia, Mary, Isabel, Jim Gordon at Barton and Christie Sts.	2.75
Proceeds of a bazaar held at the corner Silverbirch and Queen by Joan and Eileen Kelly and Betty Parkinson	14.56
No Name	5.00
In Memory of Edna	5.00
A. L. A. E. D., Midland	5.00
Joan	1.00
Proceeds of a bazaar held at 49 Humber Cres., Humber Bay, by Audrey, Maye, Bertwell and Betty Basterfield	2.37
Counter box	5.25

GETS 4-YEAR TERM FOR BRUTAL ROBBERY

Special to The Star

Hamilton, July 24.—In line with the views he expressed yesterday, that assault and robbery "are crimes which must be repressed with the sternest measures," Magistrate Burbidge to-day sentenced Christopher Slaney to four years in penitentiary. Slaney was alleged to have beaten and robbed Andrew Adam, 55, and to have left him lying semi-conscious in the ...

HOPE T... STA...

Sold Hi... Premi... H...

By ...

Ottawa, J... lins (Con... western ... credit for ... which led ... "Red" Rya... at Kingsto...

"If Ryan ... going to pu... Dundalk a... to feed," ... pressing g... lease.

"Ryan so... way. More... ed the 'pe... eron of To... were grea... eron sugge... question ... Hugh Gut... Mr. Guthr... the peniter... he sold h... them as he... self. I do... anything ... what is to...

Col. Mu... see Ryan ... when the ... will be re...

FEARS ... SWEL...

Commiss... to More ...

Propert... day adva... board of ... eral appli... erate sec... Con. McB...

"The s...

CHAPTER 10

RED 4

10

EXTERIOR: TRAIN PLATFORM: EVENING

A tall man in a dark suit walks slowly down an empty train plat-form. He takes a seat on a wooden bench, settles his small bag next to him, and waits in the evening dusk for the seven o'clock train to Toronto.

In my film, this is the first scene. It is the last time in his life—possibly the only time in his life—when Red Ryan could have made a different choice. And while it became clear almost instantly that he would not be taking life up on this remarkable, undeserved chance at redemption, it's possible to imagine, as he sat on that bench waiting for his train out of Kingston, that he at least considered the possibility—allowed the idea a moment to roll around in his head—before turning his mind back to the immediate task of getting his next lie straight before the press showed up.

But that's reality, and this is the movies.

We see a hard, settled face with small blue eyes that have seen too much staring into the distance, and hear the faint sound of children playing. It's a sound our subconscious mind recognizes a split second before our conscious one, setting up an expectation before we even realize that we are going to . . .

FLASHBACKS

EXTERIOR: INNER CITY SLUM, EARLY 1900s: DAY

A gang of young street urchins run roughshod through the streets and empty lots of their neighbourhood. A montage of devilment is shown. Apples stolen from the sidewalk in front of a fruit store. A sleeping old man's shoelaces tied together. A beat cop's nightstick carefully slipped out of his belt, leaving him looking around in all directions, scratching his head in puzzlement. One of the youngsters spots two chickens in a backyard coop. He gets an idea, turns, cups his hands around his mouth and calls loudly, "RED!"

The cutest rapscallion is Red. Our first glimpse shows him pulling a little girl's pigtails. At the sound of his name being called, he turns his soot-smudged face to see who's calling. At the sight of his friend, his face lights up in a wide smile. Red runs to his friend. They look around to make sure nobody sees them, then they each grab a chicken and run.

Looking behind them as they turn a corner, both lads run right into the comical cop, who is now holding his nightstick and looking at the boys with that warm/stern face that character actors who played beat cops in the 1930s did so well. One boy's ear held firmly in each hand, he marches them down to the precinct house.

Then follows a series of misdemeanors—shooting at cats in the dump, stealing cherries from an old woman's tree, playing hooky from school—each followed by the constable marching Red and the boys down to see the magistrate. It's all just youthful mischief. There's no cause for alarm. Just boys feeling their oats. Heck, Red will probably grow up to be a cop on the beat himself. Or a prize fighter. That's how these stories usually turn out.

But then we come to the deaf judge, with his ear horn, and the greasy lying lawyer, himself a past victim of one of the young gang's stunts. You remember from chapter 7 how that scene was reported in the *Globe*? When Red and his pals were asked about their future plans?

RED: *(Boyishly and tremblingly)* We've made up our minds to go straight, Your Honour.
DEAF JUDGE: What do they say?
EVIL PROSECUTOR: They say, Your Worship, that they will continue to live lives of crime.
DEAF JUDGE: Very well, then, five years in the penitentiary.

The flashbacks get darker now. Red in prison stripes, breaking rocks. Red in the yard, slipping contraband to another inmate. Red talking out of the side of his mouth. Getting bigger, stronger, harder.

The next time Red is free he's sticking up banks. Peeling off in getaway cars. Counting money on hotel room tables with a gun in a shoulder holster and a moll on his lap.

The next time he's caught, spinning newspapers blast front-page headlines.

- **RED RYAN CAPTURED**
- **BANDIT RYAN'S TRIAL TODAY**
- **RYAN GETS 25 YEARS**

And back to jail we go. Back to breaking rocks. And this time, planning the big prison break.

We see the break. The fire started in the barn. The smoke covering the four other convicts going up over the wall. Red staying until the last of them is over, fighting off a brutal prison guard we saw earlier terrorizing inmates, before climbing up and over himself. The mad dash on the other side of the wall. Commandeering a car. Leading police on a high-speed chase through the streets of the prison town and out into the country. The convict driving the car has been shot. He's bleeding. The car crashes into a farm gate and the men head out on foot. The man who's been shot can't go on. Red tends to him. He tries to make him comfortable as the police are seen approaching, putting his own life in danger to assist his friend.

When it comes to honour among thieves, Red Ryan takes a back seat to no one.

His friend implores Ryan to leave him: "I'm done for, Red. Save yourself." Reluctantly, he does, sprinting off towards the nearby woods, gaining on his mates and leaving the winded cops behind. The police shoot wildly at the sprinting figure, but their bullets don't hit Red Ryan.

Now the men are hiding deep in the woods. Wading through swamps. The pursuers with their dogs always circling. Days pass. And nights. Time is marked by whisker growth, muddier prison clothes and little Runty getting weaker.

Finally, the chance to steal a car and get free. A safe house. A change of clothes. Red and Curly say goodbye to Big Simpson and Runty, and it's off to America and the greatest bank-robbing spree of all time.

These are very long flashbacks. Maybe Red Ryan has gotten off the bench on the train platform by now and boarded the train. Maybe his faraway gaze is now aimed out a train window. I'm not sure how much flashbackage can be supported by the form. I'll have to re-watch *Citizen Kane*.

Robbing banks. Flashy clothes, jewellery, cars, women. Red and Curly are on a roll. The stacks of money on the hotel room tables are two feet high. Champagne flows. Until, inevitably, another shootout with the cops. Curly dead and Red, in irons, brought back to the Pen.

But this time, something is different. There is a yin to the evil lawyer's yang, in the person of the good prison priest, who sees the essential goodness still living deep inside the hardened criminal. And the old Red starts to return. The

caring hospital orderly, easing the suffering of the other prisoners. The thief who invents a thief-proof lock (be patient,
I'll explain this bit later). The hero who puts down the
prison riots singlehandedly. The convict-scholar studying
the great books in his well-kept cell, building his little light-
bulb crucifixes.

Now the newspaper headlines say something different.

- **RED RYAN STOPS PRISON RIOT**
- **RYAN A REFORMED MAN**
- **PRIME MINISTER TO CONSIDER RYAN PARDON**

And the prime minister comes to visit Ryan's cell. The two
men talk sincerely. They clearly share a bond. There is a deep
trust there. Later, in his office on Parliament Hill, we see the
prime minister writing a letter to Red's sister. And we hear it,
in voice-over:

> *I was greatly impressed by what he said to me, and I*
> *understand the priest of the institution was of the opinion*
> *that he would take your brother into his employ if he were*
> *liberated.*
>
> *The minister charged with responsibility in such matters*
> *is at the moment absent. When he returns, I will speak to*
> *him about this matter.*

Then, one rainy day, the warden visits Red's cell. "Well,
Ryan, do you think it would be too wet to go out today?" He
holds the ticket-of-leave behind his back.

"I'd go in a bathing suit," says Red, his smile shining as it hasn't since his youth.

And we're back on the train. It's July 23, 1935.

Those flashbacks are definitely too long.

DOES RYAN BELIEVE any of this story? Narcissists can apparently come to believe some pretty outrageous things about themselves. Perhaps a narcissist comes to mind who proves my point. But whether the Jesse James of Canada believes it or not, this is the story he tells.

Red Ryan was supposed to be travelling by train from Kingston to Toronto's Union Station. That's where reporters from three of the city's newspapers were waiting for him a little before midnight. But considering the fact that no reporters from the *Star* were standing with them on the platform, I have to wonder how surprised those reporters were when tomorrow's front-page attraction didn't get off the train.

In fact, Ryan left the train in Belleville, less than an hour west of Kingston, and hopped into a car with two *Star* reporters, who drove him straight to his brother's house in Toronto and spent the night writing two pages of exclusive stories. The centrepiece of that coverage was the bombshell of Red Ryan's missing letters from his wife.

Wrapped around pictures none of the other papers had—"Ryan waving his greeting to freedom as he steps from train," "The 'new' Ryan, whose cheery smiles, like this one, have brightened scores of sick men and convicts at the penitentiary," "'Red' listening to the radio in his brother's home"—was a pitiable tale of heartbreak and anguish.

You see, contained in the package of letters kept from Ryan during his imprisonment were several from his young wife, written fourteen years earlier when Ryan was on trial in Montreal. They were heartfelt expressions of love and support. According to Ryan, he never saw them. According to Ryan, not having seen the letters, he believed his wife had decided she would be better off without him, and so he never tried to contact her. According to Ryan, he was told in prison in 1927 that his wife had died. It was all too much. From the *Star* story: "'A thing like that—a thing I was never able to see or answer,' almost whispered the 40-year-old, blue-eyed man just released from Kingston."

"Brutal," said Father Kingsley, and the newspaper editorial writers could do nothing but agree. Canada's prison system, already under fire, was pilloried for its heartlessness. And Ryan's suffering only deepened his bond with the public.

It was all a crock, of course.

Within two weeks the deputy minister of justice had concluded an investigation into the letters and written to Ryan, demanding he "immediately take steps to correct the false impression in the public mind regarding correspondence with your wife." They even had a signed statement from Ryan admitting he'd seen his wife after the letters were written, and that she had written him the following year, in 1922, saying that she didn't wish to have any further communication with him.

Oh, and she wasn't dead either.

But nobody ever heard that version of events. It took McSherry to dig that stuff up fifty years later.

That day's *Star* also contained a short piece from Ottawa, where Conservative senator Colonel H.A. Mullins was patting himself on the back for being the man who got the ball rolling on Ryan's parole. He recounted how he had met Ryan while touring the Kingston Pen, had been impressed by him and had taken up the question of his parole with the justice minister. He said he planned to set Ryan up on a cattle ranch in Manitoba and "give him some steers to feed."

"I don't think you'll ever hear anything more about Ryan except what is to his credit," the colonel said. When it comes to questions of character, Canadians have always been able to turn to the Senate.

Red Ryan was the biggest thing in town, and the reporters at the *Star*, who had essentially created him, had him all to themselves. A series of front-page stories under the byline NORMAN "RED" RYAN began the next day. The first focused on his certainty that he would continue to live up to the trust others had placed in him. A certainty "as strong and enduring as life itself." He realized, he wrote, that if he didn't, he would be jeopardizing the chances of other inmates receiving the second chance he'd been given.

That story was accompanied by a colour piece reporting on Ryan's first day of freedom, a "day of bewilderment" as he walked dazed through the streets of Toronto, a city "roaring with thousands of automobiles," where streets were "a dazzle of multi-colored electric signs," and full of "the happy laughter of children at play." It was reported that he prayed at a little church, visited police headquarters, where he assured the deputy chief that "crime reaps no dividend," and joked with a reporter about opening a bank account. "Won't they get a shock when I sign my name?"

The next piece that appeared under Ryan's byline detailed his belief that half of the nation's crimes were planned in prison. It was a call for reform, particularly when it came to the incarceration of teenaged boys.

> Penitentiaries then, as now, were no places for lads of our age. . . . While there we associated with hardened criminals, some of the most vicious type, and all we heard while in prison was boasting about the "jobs" they had pulled, and what they planned to do in all channels of crime when they got out. It was a thoroughgoing school of crime.

The same day that piece ran, a letter to the editor was printed in the *Globe* recommending that, immediately after the next election, the new prime minister appoint Ryan as chief administrator of penitentiaries for Canada, "with full power to make whatever reforms he thinks best." "I do not believe there is one person who has been interested in 'Red' Ryan's case, that is not of the same opinion," wrote Alex Macpherson of Toronto. And he probably wasn't far off.

The next piece from Ryan recounted his jailhouse meeting with the prime minister. Ostensibly written as an expression of his gratitude to Bennett and the others who worked for his release, it's really just an excuse to brag: about the cleanliness of his room, about the books he was reading, about his forbearance and virtue, and, mainly, about the fact that the prime minister of Canada visited him in jail.

Roy Greenaway wrote these pieces bylined NORMAN "RED" RYAN. In his autobiography, he wrote that he liked Ryan in many ways, but always remained a little suspicious of him. Just not suspicious enough, apparently, to prevent him from writing the pieces that helped get Ryan sprung in the first place, and not suspicious enough to stop him from cranking out more self-indulgent, maudlin shite once Ryan was free. If, at any time in his life, Greenaway tried to come to terms with the rather substantial role he played in this ugly business, there is no evidence of it in his memoirs.

Jocko Thomas, who worked as a police reporter at the *Star* for sixty years, wrote at the end of his career about meeting Ryan when he was a young reporter just starting out. The story gives you a sense of just how big a deal Ryan was during those early days of freedom.

Thomas was working in the press room at police headquarters one night, shortly after Ryan's release, when Ryan came in looking for Athol Gow. Thomas and Ryan had been talking for a few minutes when the police radio went off with a fire call. As Thomas prepared to leave, Ryan asked if he could tag along. Thomas picks up the story:

> *It was often difficult for a reporter who wasn't generally known to get through fire lines. But when I approached the burning coal yard with Ryan that night, the fire line*

parted amid a flurry of handshakes from the police, who recognized my distinguished guest. It was like the arrival of a war hero. People clamored for his autograph, and the fire chief threw his arms around Red and led him close to the roaring flames, while a police sergeant bellowed at me to get away.

Back at the police station, Thomas shook hands with Ryan and noticed the hero's hand was sweaty. "It crossed my mind at the time," Thomas writes, "that people with sweaty palms should not be trusted, but I thought nothing more about it."

I think it's likely that all these old newspapermen told Ryan stories for the rest of their lives. And in all of them, I'm equally sure, they were the only ones who smelled a rat.

Ryan's time in the spotlight was limited, of course. The news items got smaller and more spread out after a couple of weeks, as the public lost interest. The *Star* ran a photo of Red posing with a judge, a city controller, Toronto's chief coroner and a well-known lawyer at the Police Athletic Association Field Day, where Red was the guest of honour. There was a small front-page item in the *Globe* in early August, reporting on Ryan's first return visit to Kingston since his release. He was the guest of honour once more, this time at a church picnic, where "with untiring friendliness, Ryan shook hands with every one." But not much after that.

I guess everyone expected Ryan to settle into something he had spent his entire life proving himself incapable of—a normal life.

———

WOULD IT SURPRISE you very much to learn that Red Ryan
didn't take Senator Mullins up on his offer of the Manitoba
cattle ranch?

No, he stayed in the city and took a job selling cars
for a dealer in the west end of town. Newspaper ads let
Torontonians know that "NORMAN 'RED' RYAN would
like to sell you your New 1935 Ford, or a Real Good Used
Car." At night, he worked for a local wrestling promoter
named Jack Corcoran. As well as putting on the big wrestling
shows at Maple Leaf Gardens, Corcoran owned a hotel on
King Street East called the Nealon House. He set Ryan up
there as a combination greeter and manager. Basically, he was
an attraction, the panda bear at the zoo. The Nealon's regulars were a sporty bunch, and Ryan was a draw. He even suggested that Corcoran hang a big banner over the door saying,
"Red Ryan is Here!" But Corcoran, apparently, didn't think
much of the idea.

THE TORONTO DAILY STAR, THURSDAY, AUGUS

NORMAN "RED" RYAN

Would like to sell you your New 1935 Ford, or a Real Good Used Car

ROSS H. FAWCETT, LIMITED

(Weston)   LY. 2123-4   JU. 1224

USED CAR RESALE DEPOT
Dundas and Pacific.   LY 1020.

Ryan was making good money. Corcoran paid him fifty dollars a week, which was a lot of money in the depths of the Great Depression. Plus he received commissions on the cars he sold. But with the media uninterested in him, there was no rush, no juice, no life. McSherry describes a typical night for Ryan at the Nealon House as sitting at a table in the beverage room, slowly sipping a beer and talking sports with the regulars. To Ryan, it must have seemed like death.

No one knows exactly how long it took for Ryan to start getting itchy for the old life. I don't think it took long at all. There was a story in the *Globe* less than a month after his release that reads like a man screaming for attention. It is short—just three paragraphs long—and it briefly states Ryan's intention to check into the whereabouts of his "lost wife." In it, I see the 1930s equivalent of a fading TV star of today telling the world he's checked into a facility to get treatment for sex addiction. Anything for some ink.

The same week as the *Globe* story, his picture appeared in the *Star*. He was working out in wrestling trunks with the professional grappler Dr. Freddy Meyers, who was training for a main event match against "Hangman" Cantonwine at Maple Leaf Gardens a couple of days later. According to the *Star*'s sports editor, Lou Marsh, Meyers tried to convince Ryan to take up wrestling himself. "'Red' didn't hesitate a second. He said, 'Nay, nay' in the most emphatic tones he could muster."

(Nay, nay?)

Red, apparently, thought wrestling was too hard on the eyes.

If Red Ryan had had an agent, he'd have been on the phone to him twice a day. "Just get me in the papers!" At any rate, a rash of bank robberies and store burglaries started in and around Toronto not long after that.

CHAPTER
11

CREEPY

11

B ack in the mid-1930s, in the heyday of the North American bank robber, only four men were designated "Public Enemy No. 1" by FBI chief J. Edgar Hoover: John Dillinger, Pretty Boy Floyd, Baby Face Nelson and Alvin Karpis. A couple of things distinguished Karpis from the other names on the list, beyond being the least well-known of the bunch. For one, he was the only one of the four to be taken alive. For another, he was the only Canadian. And while it's tough to compete against nicknames like Pretty Boy and Baby Face, Karpis had a pretty good one of his own. He was called Creepy.

Creepy Karpis was Canada's "other" famous bank robber of the 1920s and '30s. That's if you don't count old "Red"

Hamilton, the man from Sault Ste. Marie, Ontario, who, as I mentioned earlier, is best remembered for his lingering death. Karpis didn't possess Red Ryan's winning looks—in fact, he actually did look kind of creepy—or Ryan's genius for self-promotion and ability to ingratiate himself with the press boys, but Karpis made up for that by being a much better crook.

Karpis was born in Montreal in 1907. During a stint for robbery in a prison in Kansas in the 1920s, he met a fellow inmate named Fred Barker. When they got out, they hooked up with Fred's brother Doc and formed what was called at the time the Karpis-Barker gang, although history has come to know it as the Ma Barker gang.

Despite what you might have heard, Ma Barker wasn't a crook, she just had a bunch of crooked sons who took her along on their travels because it was easier to rent places to stay after pulling bank jobs if they had an older woman in the crew. They would tell the landlords they were a family on vacation. The myth of Ma Barker, criminal mastermind, was cooked up by J. Edgar Hoover after her death to justify the fact that the FBI had just shot a sixty-two-year-old woman. According to Hoover, Ma Barker was "the most vicious, dangerous and resourceful criminal brain of the last decade." According to a bank robber who knew her and her sons, she "couldn't plan breakfast."

Karpis himself wrote years later in his autobiography that, when the gang was planning a job, they'd send Ma to the movies: "Ma saw a lot of movies."

At the time, everyone knew Karpis was the brains behind

the gang, which included up to twenty-five members over the years. He was said to be highly intelligent and possessed of a photographic memory, but I'm guessing it was probably pretty easy to seem highly intelligent in a room full of Barkers. His gang robbed banks and kidnapped millionaires for ransom, netting themselves hundreds and hundreds of thousands of dollars over the course of five or six years. Eventually Fred and Ma were shot to death and Karpis was arrested, by J. Edgar Hoover himself, according to the official FBI version of things. In Karpis's version of his arrest, Hoover stayed in hiding until his officers told him it was safe to come out.

Karpis was sent to Alcatraz, where he did twenty-six years, becoming the Rock's longest-serving resident. He was transferred in 1962 to a prison in Washington state, where he did another seven years, before being released in 1969 and deported to Canada.

I'm old enough to just barely remember the media coverage when Alvin Karpis came back to Canada. I remember more clearly when, a couple of years later, his memoirs were published and he started popping up on news and interview shows talking about his gangster days. He didn't look nearly as creepy anymore, just a friendly looking grandfather type, with a grey brush cut and horn-rimmed glasses, telling stories from a time that seemed to me to be so long ago, so distant, so much another world, that he might as well have been a gunslinger from the wild west.

Karpis eventually moved to the Costa del Sol in Spain, where he died in 1979. He had spent one year of his teens, almost half of his twenties, all his thirties, his forties and his fifties, and a couple of years of his sixties behind bars. After a life like that, it's no wonder he wanted some time in the sun.

A couple of things about Karpis and his life interest me in relation to the story of Red Ryan. First of all, if you wonder what Ryan's life would have been like if that 1935 ticket-of-leave were never issued, look to Karpis. Ryan too would have gotten out eventually, especially given the fact that, without his own horrible example to foul up the system, parole reform would have happened sooner. I can see an older Red Ryan, in his sixties or seventies, writing a memoir (it would have been his third) and hitting the chat-show circuit. Obviously he would have loved the attention and, with thirty-five or forty years to polish them up, his yarns would have been fantastic, in both senses of the word. When the attention faded, as it did with Karpis and as it did with Ryan in real life, he would have been too old to return to his past life, so I can see him taking his modest book profits and setting himself up in a little apartment someplace warm. Maybe developing a drug habit to cope with the boredom, as Karpis apparently did in Spain.

So, in one way, Karpis can be seen as Ryan's "what if?" But could he have also been something more?

When Ryan was let out of prison in 1935, Karpis had already inherited the Public Enemy No. 1 mantle from Baby Face Nelson, who had been shot to death late the year before. For over half a year, Karpis had managed to elude the FBI and Hoover, and he would continue to do so for almost another full year after Ryan's release. Karpis wasn't caught until early in May 1936. That means that for almost the entire period of Ryan's freedom, as he worked to maintain the facade of his reformation and to keep his name and his face in the newspapers, Red would have been reading stories about the elusive Alvin "Creepy" Karpis, the most brilliant criminal mind in America, a Canadian who made it all the way to Public Enemy No. 1. For someone with an ego as big as Ryan's, wouldn't that have been very hard to take?

I'm not going to blame Karpis for Ryan's return to crime; that would be crazy. But I can definitely picture the Ace of Canadian Bank Robbers, about to head off to his job as a used car salesman, balling up a newspaper after reading another Karpis article, and throwing it at an inebriated Nealon House regular with a few choice profanities. I can picture him glumly thinking back to his glory days, on the run in the States, flush with cash, every paper breathlessly following every rumour about his whereabouts, and wishing he still had a little taste of what Creepy had.

ICKS FLY
DE SECTOR

FOUR IN A ROW

	A.B.	R.	H.	O.	A.
	5	0	1	1	0
1b.	5	2	1	11	1
	3	2	2	0	0
er, 2.	3	2	1	4	0
	3	2	2	1	0
2b.	5	1	3	3	7
er, ss.	5	0	1	1	1
	38	10	14	27	12

	A.B.	R.	H.	O.	A.
	4	0	2	7	4
2b.	4	0	2	7	4
ss.	4	0	1	4	4
	2	0	1	0	0
rf.	2	0	1	1	0
ush, lf.	4	1	1	5	0
	4	0	1	4	1
3b.	4	0	2	0	1
	1	0	0	0	1
	2	0	0	0	4
	34	1	9	27	15

Errors—Schulmerich, Chap-
rissey. Runs batted in—Walker
2, Richardson 2, Heffner 2,
Quinn 2, Schulmerich. Two-base
hberger. Home run—Schul-
merich. Three-base hits—Hell-
hberger. Home run—Schul-
ifices—Walker, Hershberger.
lays—Richardson to Heffner to
: Chapman to Heffner to
ouch to Morrissey; Morrissey
eft on bases—Newark 8, Toronto
s on balls—Off Hilcher 2, off
off Nekola 3. Strikeouts—By
by Nekola 3. Hits—Off Hilcher
innings (none out in fourth); off
in 6. Losing pitcher—Hilcher.
—Campbell, Sweeney and Hubbard.

ANGE A.C. NEED WIN

ght at Dovercourt park, west
should be in for the best
softball battle of the season
orange A.C. and Canada D's
their last scheduled meet-
loss for the Crushers at this
ould be very costly. Game
6.45 o'clock.

LEAGUE LEADERS

batters:
and club ... G. A.B. R. H. B.A.
Pirates .. 96 350 83 139 .397
Cards .. 103 420 91 156 .371
enters .. 102 413 83 144 .347
Indians .. 102 431 56 149 .346
Cubs .. 83 295 44 102 .346
runs: Greenberg, Tigers, 31; Ber-
ievers, 25; Ott, Giants, 24; Johnson,
21; Camilli, Phillies, 21.
atted in: Greenberg, Tigers, 127;
reves, 95; Medwick, Cardinals, 87;
s, Cardinals, 84; Ott, Giants, 84.
Medwick, Cardinals, 91; Geh-
Tigers, 91; Greenberg, Tigers, 90;
nts, 86; Galan, Cubs, 86; Gehrig,
86, Fox, Tigers, 86.
Medwick, Cardinals, 156; Terry,
153; Herman, Cubs, 150; Vosmik,
149; Cramer, Athletics, 149.

1935
HEVROLETS
ONTIACS
LDSMOBILES
UICKS
AT
PECIAL
RICES
WITH
PECIAL
ERMS

These are company
s that have been
ven a few thousand
es; all are covered
th a new-car guaran-

ACT

SPORT PARADE
by CHARLES GOOD

It will be Earl Cook-Stan Lucas
night to-night at the stadium, but
last night it was May-McQuinn-
Walker-Koy - Hershberger - Porter-
Richardson-Heffner-Duke night.

It's got so that every night is the
other fellow's night down at the
Fleet St. park and Ike Boone com-
plains that he can't do anything
about it.

☆ ☆ ☆

Boone is very bitter in the
premises. He has asked that help
be secured but nothing has been or
is being done. He intimates that he
saw the slump coming even when
they were winning and put in a
requisition for help, but all that he
got was a smile and Nekola. So
what?

☆ ☆ ☆

The Bears' win was their second
of the series and the fourth straight
defeat for the Leafs, whose hitting
was spasmodic and fielding erratic.

☆ ☆ ☆

Joe Morrissey clicked twice but
his fielding was somewhat slipshod
and it was quite evident that his
leg injury is still bothering him.
Joey missed a chance for a double
play in the first inning which, if it
had been completed, would have
retired the Bears without a run.

☆ ☆ ☆

They pushed over a Callander
count after that and Duke was king
from then on.

☆ ☆ ☆

Old Wes. Schulmerich had a
regular Buck Freeman session. He
bunted a homer out of the park,
dropped a fly ball and struck out
twice.

☆ ☆ ☆

Another veteran who was particularly prominent was "Hula Hula"
Dick Porter, who followed up his
four-hit streak of the first game by
getting two more in succession last
night and then walking twice.
Nekola finally got him out on his
ninth appearance on a bounder to
the box.

☆ ☆ ☆

Both McQuinn and Richardson
likewise distinguished themselves.
The former belted a pair of doubles
while the popular "Richie" was not
only a hitting fool but a fielding
demon. Some of his stops were
ultra sensational. He took care of
ten chances.

MINERS AND O.P.W.
BATTLE TO 2-ALL TIE

Miners and O.P.W. failed to reach
a decision in their Dentonia senior
softball fixture last night, the
score being tied two all at the end
of the ninth when darkness intervened. The Painters opened the
scoring in the second when Jimmy
Dowling walked and brother Wink
came through with a double to left.
They scored another in the third on
three successive singles, but the
Miners then came through with a
triple play to cut off the rally.
The Painters had the winning run
on base in the ninth with nobody
out, but some fast thinking by Hall
started a double play to end the
game.

WITH PICK AND SHOVEL

(Continued from Previous Page)
left two of their Cornwall silver-
ware prizes as additional security
for the gasoline needed for the car
he was in. That's a classic of
poverty, isn't it?

☆ ☆ ☆

This isn't the first time that the
Laurels have brought international
honor and glory to their native city
on this haphazard manner of travelling. It's the winning that counts
with them. But, it is the first time
that they have found it necessary
to make a public appeal to the
sportsmen of this city to help them
out of their difficulties. They are
in the hole for about $75 borrowed
here and there to pay for the meals,
lodgings, gas and oil, and those unexpected car troubles.

I'll promise to go up and sit on

"RED" RYAN TAKES TO THE MAT GAME

Norman "Red" Ryan is a busy individual these days. He sells motor
cars, manages the Nealon House hotel and in between finds time for
daily exercises. Keenly interested in wrestling after attending two
shows, he has been working out this week with Dr. Freddy Meyers who
is to oppose Howard "Hangman" Cantonwine at Maple Leaf Gardens,
Thursday night. "Red" says that wrestling is okay as a means of
keeping fit but as a profession it is too hard on the eyes, especially
against a man like Meyers.

Few
Hours of
Fame

CHAPTER
12
RED 5

12

Desperate for action, Red hooked up once again with his fellow Kingston escapee Ed "Wyoming" McMullen, who had been paroled the year before Ryan and was living in the east end of Toronto. McMullen was once described by the warden at Kingston as the most dangerous man in the penitentiary, and was, according to Peter McSherry, feared even by Ryan himself.

The third member of the team was a career crook named Harry Checkley. The *Star* called him a hardened criminal. McSherry called him a down-and-out rounder. Martin Robin called him a punk. Greenaway, in his memoirs, a thug. Rasky didn't mention Checkley in his book, which is a shame when you consider the nickname potential. But the *Globe* took care of that problem for us—posthumously, unfortunately for Checkley. Quoting Ryan's brother Russ, the *Globe* reported that the bandit was known as Chuck.

That's right. Chuck Checkley.

His arrest sheet included convictions for burglary, theft, indecent assault and carrying a concealed weapon. His most recent appearance in court before hooking up with Ryan and McMullen came after he was caught stealing eleven pairs of socks.

This was the Red Ryan gang.

McSherry figures Ryan was back to his old tricks by October, three months after he was released. "He never intended otherwise," McSherry writes, as I have mentioned before.

A liquor store, a bank, an office, a produce company—the common thread was the use of nitroglycerine to blow open the safes. There were so many of these nitro jobs that a special police squad was formed. There were old fashioned bank hold-ups as well. One in Toronto. One in Hamilton that followed the Ryan style so closely the local paper reported the bandits had "modelled their tactics after those used by the . . . ace of Canadian holdup men," the famous Red Ryan.

Ryan's generous Christmas gifts that year resulted in an informant whispering in the ear of a Toronto police inspector that he should be keeping an eye on the Golden Boy of Crime. When the inspector scoffed at the idea, pointing out that Ryan was making plenty of money legitimately, the informant said, "Not as much as he's spending."

I'm going to present a set piece now, but before I do, I'd like you to keep in mind as you read this that while these events were transpiring, Red Ryan and his old friend Dr. Oswald Withrow, the ex-con who wrote the glowing *Globe* piece in which he compared Ryan to "David of sacred history," were lobbying to have Ryan appointed to a new Royal Commission charged with investigating conditions in Canada's penitentiaries. Withrow was also polishing up Ryan's prison manuscript, "The Futility of Crime," for publication. The two men had agreed to split the proceeds fifty-fifty.

So it came to pass that the Ryan gang needed a fast getaway car, and Red had seen one in Markham, a small town northeast of Toronto. They drove their old Ford out to the country and, at three thirty in the morning of a snowy February 29—leap day—Ryan, McMullen and Checkley broke into the garage where the big Chevrolet was kept by its owner, Edward Stonehouse.

The boys didn't know it, but they'd tripped an alarm when they broke into the garage, waking up Stonehouse and his twenty-four-year-old son, James. The two men called the police and got dressed, and then, just as McMullen gunned the stolen car out of the garage, the Stonehouse men ran out of their house and jumped on the running board, trying to stop the theft in progress. As Edward Stonehouse tried to force his way in the passenger door, McMullen pulled out his revolver and shot the car owner in the head. With the elder Stonehouse slumped over in the front seat, McMullen fired at the son, who was trying to follow his father into the car. The first shot hit James Stonehouse in the hand, but he kept coming. The second shot hit James in the stomach, but that still wasn't enough to stop him. He started choking and beating on McMullen, knocking out two of the driver's teeth, and eventually forced him to stop the car just outside of town. With McMullen beaten almost senseless, James Stonehouse grabbed the car keys and threw them out into a snowbank.

At this point, Ryan and Checkley showed up. They'd been following the stolen car in their Ford. Ryan got out and pointed a shotgun at the wounded younger Stonehouse. Thinking he was about to get shot again, he pulled his father's body out of the Chev and attempted to escape from the robbers. But he didn't get far, collapsing into the snow that filled the ditch next to the road.

Standing over the two men with his shotgun, Ryan yelled at them for the missing keys. Getting no answer, he slammed the butt of the shotgun into Edward Stonehouse's head. Then the author of "The Futility of Crime" grabbed a flashlight and started frantically looking for the keys in the snow.

All this noise had woken up a teenaged boy who lived across the road. When he went outside and asked what was going on, Ryan pointed his shotgun and told the kid to get away, which he quickly did. But this was enough to convince the men that they had better get going, even if that meant leaving their newly acquired Chev.

After piling into the Ford and driving a few hundred yards, according to McSherry, McMullen and Ryan got into an argument. McMullen wanted to go back and make sure both men were dead. And if they weren't, he wanted to kill them. He didn't want any live witnesses. Ryan was against the idea. He just wanted to get away. It was at this point that the police, in the person of Constable James Walker, arrived on the scene. You'll remember that the Stonehouse men had called them before trying to stop the robbery themselves.

Spotting Walker's headlights coming up fast, Ryan and McMullen ended their argument, got out of the car, and started pumping shotgun and revolver shots in the direction of the cop. This forced Walker to stop his car, get out and find cover behind it. And that gave the robbers the time they needed to get back in their car and speed away, hightailing it back to Toronto.

Edward Stonehouse was dead. His son, James, was seriously wounded.

It must be said that this version of events isn't the only one out there. Most versions have Ryan shooting the younger Stonehouse. In fact, that's the conclusion that a report prepared for the attorney general of Ontario came to later that year: that McMullen killed the father and Ryan wounded the son. But this version has the feel of the truth, and it's the one McSherry settled on.

However it went down, a couple of days later Ryan offered his services to Toronto police, saying he'd be willing to go undercover to help track down the Stonehouse killers. He had a set of balls on him.

THERE'S ONLY ONE more story to tell after the Markham shootings, but since it's the last one, I'm not really in any hurry to get there. So let's jump ahead to March 1939, three years after the Markham shootings. The *Star*'s headline says VICTIM OF "RED" RYAN J.E. STONEHOUSE DIES. And the story reads:

> James E. Stonehouse, Markham garage
> operator, died last night in his 28th
> year. Three years ago he was wounded
> and his father, E.A. Stonehouse, was
> murdered, as they attempted to stop
> three thieves from escaping with a
> car stolen from the garage.

James had suffered heart attacks
during the past year and passed
away after a short illness. Only his
mother and four sisters remain to
carry on the business.

Norman "Red" Ryan and his gang
were blamed by police for the shooting three years ago.

A horrible, senseless death, reported in the same newspaper
that bore so much responsibility for causing it.

BACK IN TORONTO in 1936 the Ryan gang was getting very
nervous. If they were fingered for the Stonehouse murder,
it would be the gallows for all three. McMullen, in particular, was obsessed with the idea that James Stonehouse could
identify him. The men decided they'd head to the west coast
after pulling a couple of jobs to finance the move. They bungled a bank robbery in St. Thomas, Ontario, west of Toronto.
They bungled a couple of night-time robberies north of the
city. They managed to pull off one safecracking job. And they
successfully withdrew about $3,500 from a bank in Quebec.

But people were talking. Even Father Kingsley was getting suspicious. He'd received an anonymous letter claiming
Ryan was robbing banks and running around with women.
When he showed the note to Ryan, Ryan recognized the
handwriting of one of his sisters. Needless to say, he denied
everything.

Around the same time as the letter surfaced, a prostitute friend of Ryan's told him that another girl who worked out of a brothel in downtown Toronto had confidently told her that Red Ryan had committed the Markham murder.

This was more than enough for Ed McMullen, who packed up his stuff and headed west to Vancouver. But Ryan couldn't leave. His parole conditions required that he check in regularly with the Toronto police. He knew it was just a matter of time before he was picked up and questioned about the Markham murder. He tried to get the conditions of his parole changed. When that failed, he told police he was heading out on a fishing trip for a few weeks, to buy himself some time.

All he needed to do now was pull one last job to cover his travel costs. A piece of cake for the ace of Canadian holdup men and his sidekick, Chuck Checkley.

THERE WERE TWO separate doors in front of the liquor store on Christina Street in downtown Sarnia, Ontario. One was marked IN, the other marked OUT. That's important. When you went in the IN door, a few steps led you up to a landing where a door let you in to the store itself. Leaving the store was the same procedure, but on the other side, using the OUT door. While the two doors were right next to each other on the street, the two vestibules inside were not connected. In other words, if you went in the IN door, you couldn't just come right out the OUT door. You'd have to go up the stairs, cross through the store, and then come down the OUT stairs on the other side. That's important too.

May 23, 1936, was the Saturday of a long weekend. The liquor store would be closed on both Sunday and Monday. The plan was to hit the store right at six o'clock, closing time, just after the last customers left and just as the tills were bursting with the holiday weekend receipts.

That was the plan. But two little wrinkles messed it up.

Ryan and Checkley slipped in through the entrance door a couple of minutes before six. They were dressed in railway overalls. Once inside, they locked the IN door behind them and waited at the bottom of the stairs for the customers inside to finish up and leave through the separate OUT door.

But inside the store, a customer named Austin Glass had discovered he was twenty-five cents short of the price of his purchase, and not seeing anyone in the store he wanted to approach for a loan, he peeked down into the entrance stairs to see if there was a friend coming up who would help him out. What he saw was two railway men in the process of covering their faces with handkerchiefs. Glass saw the robbers, and the robbers saw Glass. So much for waiting for the store to clear.

Ryan and Checkley sprang into action, or as the *Globe* put it on Monday's front page, "Quickly their slow, careless attitude changed to the slinking litheness of a cat."

They pounded up the stairs, yelling, "Stick 'em up!" But now they were dealing with more than just the staff. There were about twenty-five customers in the place as well. Things were not going to go as smoothly as expected.

After making sure Checkley had the customers covered, and the customers had their hands up and were facing the rear wall, Ryan vaulted the counter—a patented move of his—and began emptying the cash drawers. Around this time the second piece of bad luck occurred, although given how badly this job was planned and executed, putting it all down to bad luck is probably a mistake.

Two last-minute customers showed up at the store and discovered that the IN door was locked. What Ryan and Checkley didn't know—and store regulars did—was that the OUT door could be pried open from the sidewalk. Facing a long, dry weekend, that's exactly what the men did. As they climbed the stairs into the store unseen, they noticed the group of customers standing with their backs to them and their hands up. One of the men caught the eye of a clerk standing behind the counter, realized what was happening and pulled his companion back down the stairs—still unseen by the robbers—and out the door. The men ran to a nearby taxi stand and reported the robbery to a driver, who called the police.

In less than a minute, four Sarnia policemen were on the scene.

At this point in the story, McSherry has Ryan lingering in the liquor store. "Lingering too long as usual" is how he puts it. Then, after deciding he had all the money and it was time to go, McSherry's Ryan changes his mind and lingers some more, moving the staff and customers back and forth across the store.

It's possible he was trying to herd the customers back towards the rear of the store, where it would take them longer to leave and sound the alarm, but I think the "lingering" description probably fits. This was really where Red Ryan wanted to be. If slowly sipping beers with the regular customers at the Nealon House was death, this was life. As long as he stayed in the liquor store, pointing a gun at the staff and customers, he was what he always believed himself to be: the biggest man in the room, the centre of gravity around whom all others revolved.

But the lingering time was over.

Ryan heard a noise on the stairs. It was the four Sarnia policemen, charging up through the OUT door. They were led by a thirty-three-year-old constable named John Lewis, who had been on the force for seven years. He was married with two young children. When he reached the top of the stairs, Ryan pumped four shots into his chest.

Now all hell broke loose. The customers and staff bolted for whatever cover they could find. Ryan started firing at the next cop coming up the steps, but was hit himself, in the left arm. Ryan could see his escape route down the OUT door stairs was blocked by the police, so he turned and ran towards the IN door stairway, where Checkley was still standing, as if frozen. Both Ryan and Checkley were hit by police fire, but they did make it into the stairwell, where they found themselves not just wounded, but trapped. One police officer ran back out the OUT door and took up a position on the sidewalk, ready to fire if the bandits made it out. The other two officers who were able—Lewis was being attended to by customers—stood protected by the wall at the top of the stairwell. One of them reached his revolver around the corner and fired at will down the stairs until he ran out of bullets. Then the other officer started doing the same.

How Ryan and Companio

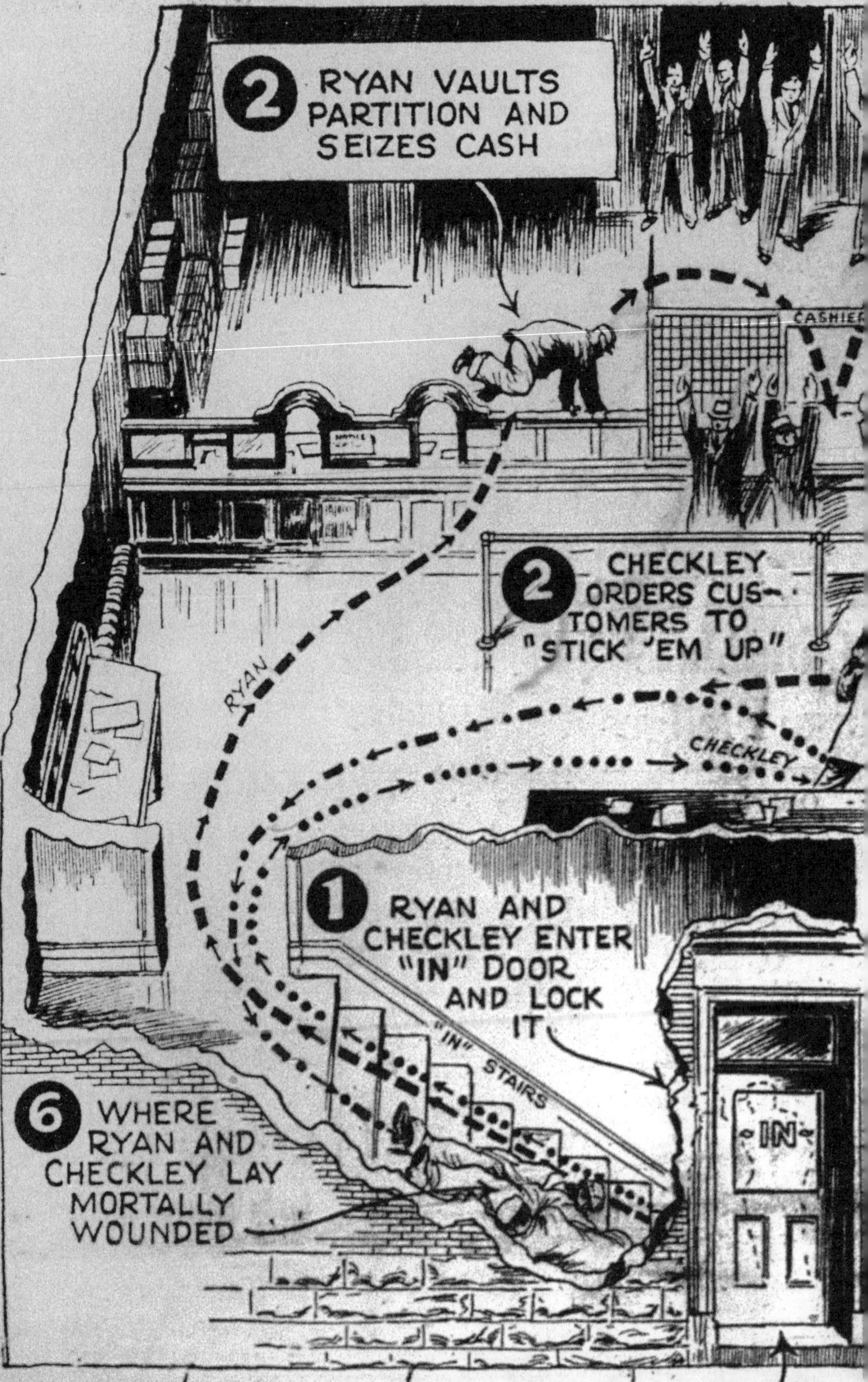

Staged Their Last Crime

3 RYAN COMES THROUGH GATE TO JOIN COMPANION

5 RYAN and CHECKLEY RETREAT TO "IN" STAIRS AS OTHER POLICE OPEN FIRE.

4 RYAN SHOOTS DOWN CONSTABLE LEWIS

Ryan kept firing up the stairwell while trying to unlock the door he himself had locked just a few minutes before, but it didn't last long. In a matter of seconds, both men were badly shot up. Checkley, halfway down the stairs, dropped his guns, raised his hands, said, "I give up," according to one of the policemen who did the shooting, and fell backwards down the stairs. Ryan threw his guns up to the top of the stairs, said nothing, according to the cop, and collapsed in the vestibule, between Checkley and the door.

Ryan always referred to the criminal life as "the game." It was now over.

Checkley was probably already dead on the stairs. Constable Lewis made it to the hospital and died about half an hour later, after being able to spend a very brief last moment with his wife in which, according to her, he had the strength to utter one last sentence: "I guess I'll soon be with Mr. Rhoades," a reference to a friend who had just died.

Ryan lasted about an hour after that. The fatal shot had hit him in the right temple.

If Ryan's life passed before his eyes at the end, chances are it didn't look very much like the flashbacks that opened chapter 10. His real life was made up of lies, betrayals, cowardice and violence. That's how it ended, with the killing of John Lewis, and that's how it began, as the "malicious little bastard" stealing bikes and chickens on the streets of Toronto.

As he was dying in the Sarnia hospital, the police went through Ryan's pockets looking for some identification papers

THIS LICENSE MUST BE CARRIED BY OPERATOR
NOT VALID TO OPERATE A MOTOR VEHICLE AS A

1936 No. 121238
MOTOR VEHICLE OPERATOR'S LICENSE
PROVINCE OF ONTARIO
T. B. McQUESTEN, MINISTER OF HIGHWAYS

ISSUED PURSUANT TO PART XII OF THE HIGHWAY TRAFFIC ACT. THIS LICENSE WHEN SIGNED BY THE OPERATOR
IS VALID UNTIL DEC. 31st 1936 AND MUST BE PRESENTED FOR RENEWAL ANNUALLY

SIGNATURE OF OPERATOR — O OR R — R

NAME JOHN N. RYAN SEX M
STREET AND NUMBER 279 LANSDOWNE AVE
CITY, TOWN OR POST OFFICE TORONTO AGE 40
COUNTY YORK
APPLICATION FOR 1937 RENEWAL ON REVERSE HEREOF

O.P.C. 2 | OFFICE No 3 | DATED JAN 30 | COUNTERSIGNED Bickell
REGISTRAR OF MOTOR VEHICLES

①

TRANSFER OF MOTOR VEHICLE PERMIT (PASSENGER)
1936 No. E2431
PROVINCE OF ONTARIO
T. B. McQUESTEN, MINISTER OF HIGHWAYS

ISSUED FOR THE FOLLOWING DESCRIBED VEHICLE

MAKE OF VEHICLE	MODEL	No OF CYL	H. P	
YEAR Chrysler 32	C+	6	25.3	FEE PAID $2.00
STYLE	SERIAL NUMBER	ENGINE NUMBER	COLOUR	
Bds	9754131	C17125	Grey	

No. 3625

To Norman J. Ryan
279 Lansdowne Ave,
Toronto, Ont.
COUNTY
APPLICATION FOR 1937 RENEWAL ON REVERSE HEREOF

C.D. 8 | OFFICE No H.O. | DATED Apr 20 | COUNTERSIGNED Bickell

②

for the robber they'd been calling "the big man." They found a motor vehicle permit issued to Norman J. Ryan.

Then a whole new kind of hell broke loose.

CHAPTER 13

TORONTO THE GOOD

13

Christ, I hate to leave Paris for Toronto.

—Ernest Hemingway

The Polish physicist Leopold Infeld had a remarkable
life. Albert Einstein's great collaborator was born in the
Jewish ghetto of Krakow in 1898. After receiving his doctorate
in theoretical physics in 1921—the first such doctorate ever
awarded by a Polish university—he found himself, as a Jew,
unable to find an academic posting. He was finally forced to
accept a position teaching at a high school in the small Polish
town of Konin, where he worked for two years before landing a spot teaching physics at a Jewish gymnasium for girls
in Warsaw. Finally, in 1930, more than eight years after his
doctorate was awarded, he received an academic posting in

Ukraine. But when his wife died two years later, he accepted a grant to study at Cambridge.

In England, he collaborated with Max Born. One result of that collaboration was the Born-Infeld model of electro-dynamics, which is still used today in the study of string theory. But, while the work was productive, his social life was not—he had a brief, unsuccessful marriage—and so in 1935 he returned to Ukraine, just in time for the Nazi threat to convince him that remaining in Europe was no longer an option.

With Einstein's support, Infeld received a grant to con-tinue his work at Princeton, and it was there, in the years 1936–1938, that the collaboration between Einstein and Infeld took place. The two physicists co-wrote the popular science text *The Evolution of Physics,* and formulated the equation that describes the movements of stars.

In 1938, Leopold Infeld accepted a professorship at the University of Toronto. He would remain in Toronto through-out the war years, until 1950. He would marry there, and he and his wife, Helen, would have two children.

For a Polish Jew, Toronto in the early 1940s might have seemed like a slice of paradise, particularly when you consider some of the alternatives. And yet, this is what Infeld wrote about his adopted city in his 1941 autobiography, *Quest:*

> *It must be good to die in Toronto. The transition between life and death would be continuous, painless and scarcely noticeable in this silent town. I dreaded the Sundays and prayed to God that if He chose for me to die in Toronto He*

would let it be on a Saturday afternoon, to save me from
one more Toronto Sunday.

Welcome to Toronto the Good.

In February 1912, Toronto City Council passed a bylaw outlawing tobogganing in public parks on Sundays. The bylaw stayed on the books until 1961. There were a lot of things you couldn't do in Toronto on Sunday.

You couldn't work. At all. Farm workers, labourers, mechanics, drivers, bakers, barbers—they were all specifically prohibited from working. You couldn't conduct business. That included buying or selling anything, with a very few exceptions, such as milk (for domestic use only) and medicine. No contracts could be entered into. No newspapers delivered.

Obviously, everything fun was outlawed. So no games, races or other sporting events. The Sunday laws of 1911 specifically prohibited events "which are noisy, or at which a fee is charged" and "the business of amusement or entertainment." All excursions "with the object of pleasure" were banned, be they "by train, steamer or other conveyance." You couldn't gamble, drink or use profane language. No public meetings were permitted, except church services, of course. You couldn't hunt, shoot or fish, or advertise anything unlawful that was taking place on a Sunday, "either in Canada or across the line." Finally, you couldn't bathe on Sunday "in any public place or in sight of a place of public worship, or private residence."

The penalties for breaking any of these Lord's Day laws ranged from one dollar to five hundred dollars.

Oh, and one other thing: playground swings in city parks were padlocked by Toronto police every Sunday, just to be on the safe side.

Sabbatarianism wasn't nearly as much fun as the name suggests. The idea was to uphold what was called at the time "the English Sunday," the proposition that everyone needed one day set aside each week purely for the contemplation of their moral and spiritual selves. So, if potatoes needed peeling for Sunday dinner, those potatoes should be peeled on Saturday. As the historian John Grant wrote about Sabbatarianism's peak in the late 1800s, "Even the irreligious went to church on Sunday; the religious went more than once," and "a great many Canadians spent the rest of the sabbath [sic] reading religious books or periodicals."

It was a Protestant thing. Catholics were much more laid back when it came to Sundays. And Toronto was a Protestant town. Orange Lodges, the Glorious Twelfth, all that.

Morley Callaghan wrote that, intellectually and spiritually, he felt like an alien in his native city. He was Catholic, for one thing. He described himself also as "intensely North American" because of his love of baseball, boxing and women. Toronto was, he wrote, fundamentally British.

When Hemingway rolled into town in the 1920s, Sabbatarianism was still in full swing. He called Toronto "the City of Churches." In a letter to Ezra Pound, he complained that the rules surrounding the sale of alcohol in town—purchasers required a doctor's note—meant he hadn't had a drink in five days, a state of affairs that prevented him from sleeping and made him feel like crying.

Michael Reynolds, in his book *Hemingway: The Paris Years*, begins his chapter about Ernest and his wife Hadley's time in Toronto by writing, "They went to Toronto to have a baby, planning to stay a year, maybe two. They only lasted four months. Four months was a long time in Toronto."

As Infeld found, the Sunday laws were still in place in the 1940s. Another visitor to Toronto during the war years was the British artist and critic Wyndham Lewis, who described the city as a "sanctimonious icebox." "If New York is brutal and Babylonian," he wrote, "in this place it is as if some one were sitting on your chest—having taken the care to gag you first—and were croaking out [hymns] . . . from dawn to dayshut."

Toronto's first cocktail lounge, the Silver Rail, didn't open until 1947.

This isn't just ancient history.

When the Toronto Blue Jays began playing in 1977, no beer was sold at their home park, Exhibition Stadium. The province wouldn't allow it, and the city didn't object. And the team was owned by a brewery. There was no beer sold at Maple Leaf Gardens for hockey either.

When I started working in restaurants, back in the late 1970s, cellophane-wrapped sandwiches were kept in the fridge behind the bar for Sunday customers. Nobody ate them; they were just put on the tables because the liquor laws didn't allow bar patrons to drink on Sunday, unless they were also eating. I remember one place that had us ring in a two-dollar rum and coke at the cash register as one dollar for the rum under LIQUOR and one dollar for the coke under FOOD.

But all that was positively progressive, compared to the stifling Presbyterian reality that hit Red Ryan square in the face every day of his life in Toronto. It was a reality that he understood very well, and learned to work to his advantage.

I WENT LOOKING for Red Ryan one Sunday on King Street in Toronto.

Let me back it up a little.

First, I went looking for Peter McSherry.

According to notes at the end of his biography of Ryan, *The Big Red Fox*—which, if I haven't mentioned it before, I recommend very much—McSherry first heard Ryan's name as a young boy in the early 1950s. He was listening to two men on the radio with names that will be familiar to old Torontonians:

Jack Dennett, the long-time announcer on CFRB and *Hockey Night in Canada,* and the old Toronto Maple Leaf winger Harold "Baldy" Cotton.

I don't know why they were talking about Ryan; McSherry doesn't say, but hearing about the famous crook piqued his interest. McSherry's father filled in more details of Ryan's story. His father also told him that he had known the bank robber and that he, along with several of McSherry's aunts and uncles, had gone to school with some of Ryan's brothers and sisters. Other neighbours provided him with more information, and an almost lifelong (I don't want to call it an obsession, because McSherry doesn't) . . . mission was seeded.

McSherry wrote his book between 1977 and 1998; it took him twenty-one years. During that time he drove a cab. In fact, it was while driving a cab that he says he met several of his best sources of information. I picture him bringing up the subject of Red Ryan regularly with passengers of a certain age, particularly if they looked like they'd lived hard.

His wasn't a leisurely life of letters. In his thank-yous, one couple is thanked for housing and feeding him for five weeks while he conducted research in Ottawa. Another woman is thanked for two weeks of hospitality. Several friends are thanked for lending McSherry money and listening to him "rant on and on about a bank robber for years." The final words of the Acknowledgements are "The book was researched and written entirely without a grant of any kind, which was important to me. I won't explain why."

I want to meet up with this guy.

He wrote two other books after the Ryan one, a memoir and a biography of another criminal, which came out in 2013. All three were published by the same company, but it had no contact information for him when I asked. A very helpful person at his publishing house told me it was extremely unusual to lose contact with a current author like that.

I found two articles he'd written in the past couple of years about the taxi industry for a Toronto neighbourhood newspaper. But the contact information on the paper's website is out of date and the phone number has been disconnected. (In fact, I later discovered the publication has been investigated by the hate crimes unit of Toronto police for anti-Semitism. McSherry's contributions seem to be just about taxis.)

Beyond those few scraps, and some archived interviews from back when the Ryan book came out, nothing.

I'd like to talk to him about Ryan, of course. I'd be very surprised if he stopped accumulating information about the man after the book was printed. I don't think you can turn off a lifelong labour that easily. And I'd also like to talk to McSherry about himself. What was it about Ryan's story that so completely captivated him? What was it that drove him for all those years? I picture him and me driving through the west-end neighbourhood where both he and Ryan lived. Talking about the past. The ghosts.

But then again, maybe it's a good thing I can't find McSherry. I know I just wrote that I'm reluctant to call his work an obsession, but judging by the almost two pages of footnotes explaining the efforts he put into nailing down the address of the house where Ryan spent the first four years of his life, he might be a little too detail-focused for my work. The house was on Augusta Avenue, which was called Esther Street at the time. The clincher for McSherry was an article written by Tommy Levine of the *Evening Telegram*, reminiscing after Ryan's death about a conversation he'd had with the bandit. Levine wrote that Ryan told him he was born in a house near Queen and Palmerston. He also told Levine about a gunfight his old pal Art Conley had had with police at Queen and Augusta. But since everyone knew the gunfight had taken place at Queen and Palmerston, McSherry writes, "it is reasonable to conclude that Levine reversed the locations associated with these two events."

You can't argue with that.

The Augusta house is long gone. A nondescript two-storey red-brick duplex sits there now. There is a stone yard on one side, gravel on the other, the yards separated by a crumbling concrete path leading to the front steps. Two small vegetable gardens, each wrapped in chicken wire, hug the sidewalk on each side of the path.

A house on Markham Street came later, but it too is gone now. In its place is a well-maintained sixties-style semi, red brick with light wood accents.

By the time the Ryan family moved to Parkdale and became approximate neighbours of the McSherrys, Red was seventeen years old and making his first appearances in the newspapers. So, chances are, he wasn't spending too much time *en famille*.

That's why I went looking for Red Ryan on King Street, where the Nealon House still stands, four floors of red brick with stone detailing, built in what the experts would call the Romanesque revival style, and I would describe as Late Victorian Pile.

It's no longer occupied, but was fairly recently (by the look of it) an auction house. I base that guess on the relatively small number of flies I counted on the windowsill visible from the sidewalk. A sandwich board leaning against the inside of the front window says AUCTION PREVIEW TODAY. And a small sign attached to the front of the building offers customers both Cash for Gold and Loans.

It looks to be in good shape.

On the west side of the building, high up near the roof, you can still make out some of the old Nealon House sign, painted on the brick. The *N*, *E* and *A* were still visible when I visited. To the left of the main door, as you face the building, is a separate door at the top of a few stairs that leads to the higher floors, where an antique store used to be located. On the higher of the two glass door panes, peel-and-stick gold letters that aren't even close to being centred spell out Beethoven Hall. And above the door, in a fancy framed nook behind the glass transom, sits a bust of Beethoven. At least I assume it's a bust of Beethoven. It certainly looks like a bust of Beethoven. Whether it looks like the actual Beethoven, I couldn't say.

That's the thing with busts of Beethoven, it isn't necessary that they look like Beethoven, only that they look like other busts of Beethoven.

The large front room that's visible through the street windows looks nothing like it would have when Ryan held court there. It's been stripped pretty bare. The walls have been sandblasted down to their yellow brick roots. The floor is a dusty honey oak. A large counter can be seen across the rear wall, but it looks like a fairly recent construction, a wide plank top resting on what looks like a stack of four-by-fours. I'm sure Ryan would recognize the exterior, but there are no signs of him, his life or his times inside.

Legend has it there are bullet holes in the front wall of the Nealon House basement, from Red Ryan's target practice.

THERE WAS NOTHING particularly remarkable about Red Ryan other than the facts of his life. He was constantly being described as a charming rogue by newspaper reporters, but I don't think any of them, really, had any idea what "charming" meant. The quotes attributed to him—whether he really said them or not—were more often than not the kind of banal, automatic wisecrack you would get from that tiresome friend of your father's, the one who was always telling you how much he knew the score. When the Golden Boy was being serious, his default mode alternated between maudlin and faux-modest.

Ryan embodied everything Torontonians abhorred. He refused honest work. He ignored the Sabbath. He drank, stole and ran around with loose women. He lied constantly. When wearing his country's colours, he showed himself to be a coward. And yet, despite all that, he had his city eating out of his hand. He was their "pet boy" and they loved him.

I suspect it was some combination of his nickname, his clean-cut face in the newspaper photos, the fact he escaped from the unbreakable Kingston Pen and probably a dash of his success robbing banks in the big leagues south of the border. He also had a phenomenal public relations team.

As well, perhaps Ryan understood something about his hometown that Emma Goldman saw as well. The anarchist and writer, who lived out her final years in exile in Toronto, called her place of refuge "deadly dull." When she was asked by a reporter to explain what she meant, she said, "Because it's church-ridden. Toronto people are smug and don't think for themselves." The smugness and incapacity for original thinking were qualities that Red Ryan understood. And even if he wouldn't have been able to articulate it, he knew precisely how to manipulate them. Once Torontonians come to accept the truth of a thing, that's the end of all inquiry. Any group of people who could be convinced that their God wanted playground swing sets padlocked on Sundays could be convinced of anything.

Ryan knew that as long as he continued to give his city the appearance of reformation, even barely, he could carry on however he pleased, because the unthinking crowd simply wouldn't see anything that contradicted their beliefs. He didn't have to actually *be* a reformed criminal, he just had to act like one.

A resemblance to the actual Beethoven was not required.

———

I'D LIKE TO conclude this brief snapshot of my hometown by finishing up the story of Leopold Infeld. I mentioned that he left Toronto in 1950, but didn't say why.

After the atomic bombs were dropped on Japan in 1945, Infeld's lifelong pacifism intensified. Along with Einstein, he became a committed and vocal peace activist, and as a result, became a person of interest to the branch of the Royal Canadian Mounted Police tasked with pouring gasoline on the fire of Canadians' anti-communist paranoia. In 1950, based on nothing but rumour, Canada's Parliament denounced Infeld as a traitor who was preparing to hand over nuclear secrets to the Russians, despite the fact that he was neither a communist nor a nuclear physicist. His picture was splashed across the front pages of Canada's newspapers. His Canadian citizenship, and that of his two Canadian-born children, was revoked. According to Infeld's granddaughter, they are the only natural-born Canadians to ever have their citizenship stripped.

He returned to Poland and spent the remainder of his life teaching at the University of Warsaw, where he was described as "an inspired, and inspiring teacher," publishing over forty papers and co-writing the book *Motion and Relativity*.

In 1995, almost thirty years after his death, the University of Toronto tried to make amends, posthumously granting Infeld the title of professor emeritus.

By then, Sundays in Toronto had improved, somewhat.

IT'S TEMPTING TO consider Red Ryan's betrayal of his towns-people's trust as a kind of poetic justice, a karmic rebalancing of their betrayal of Leopold Infeld, but, of course, the Ryan story came first, so that doesn't really work. We'll just have to content ourselves with the thought that, in Red Ryan, Toronto received exactly the hero it deserved, the only kind of hero available to the sanctimonious and the judgmental— an empty one.

In the late 1920s, Toronto's chief of police, a former military man named Dennis Draper, assigned some of his constables to attend theatrical performances at the Royal Alexandra Theatre. Their job was to stand in the wings with stop-watches, timing the kisses on stage. If a kiss lasted longer than twenty seconds, the curtain would be brought down. A few years later, police again involved themselves in the doings at the Royal Alex, this time in a dramaturgical capacity, cutting the words "bathroom" and "damn" from the play *Reunion in Vienna,* and shortening a kiss in that production from eight seconds to three.

RED RYAN, PAL, OFFICER ARE SH

Three Shot Dead in Sarnia Liquor Store H

ARABS KILL BRITISH SOLDIER

SEVEN DROWN WHEN 2 BOATS ARE CAPSIZED

Markham Murder Is Laid to Ryan

Collingwood, St. Thomas, Alias Chris Robberies Also Credited to Dead Gunman

WESSENGER REPEATS ON THEFT TOUR

Goes to Tillsonburg From Guelph—Enters Same Places

SECOND CAR STOLEN

NAZIS DENIED SACRAMENTS IN HOLLAND

Catholic Clergy Join to Halt Spread of Movement

LOSS OF $175,000 IN CHURCH FIRE

Ryan Kills Polic Before Bullet Ends Career o

NORMAN ("RED") RYAN, reformed public
enemy, twelve bitter years behind prison bars, that h
and narrow, was slain on Saturday night in
police.

He was the victim of a trap sprung by his own
hold-up of a liquor store.

The last-ditch stand of Ontario's pet bay was
Red shot a courageous young Sarnia constable name
before the policeman could lift his gun.

The other victim of that three-minute blaz
armed policemen and the two daredevil desperad
dit companions. Tonight he was still unidentified
ward McMullen, London, Ont., bank bandit, Ryan's
tional prison break at Kingston in 1922, or his fan
McMullen, alias Leggett.

COMPANION DIES

HARDLY A YE

WAS FURI

PLANNED

RED IS DE

FINGERPRINTS MATCH RYAN'S

Sarnia, May 24 (CP)—Globe in

SAFE-BLOWING EQUIPMENT FOUND IN RYAN'S GARAGE

Coronation Day

May 27, 1937, Said Date Set by Cabinet

KING EDWARD VIII Coronation will take place on
May 27, 1937, the Cabinet Bureau predicted today.

Hundreds Of R

CHAPTER
14

RED 6

14

Special to the Star
Sarnia, May 25—Norman "Red" Ryan,
gunman and thug, had the life shot
out of him here Saturday night in a
pistol fight with two local officers,
who had never before drawn their guns
in the line of duty.

For the body of Red Ryan, the immediate aftermath of the
liquor store shootout involved being placed on public display,
next to the body of the still-unidentified Harry Checkley, in the
parlour of a Sarnia funeral home the following day. The two

men were naked, lying on tables, with sheets pulled up to their waists. Some reports say the sheets were gold. Some say Ryan's was silver-grey and Checkley's brown. Some don't mention a colour at all. It's believed about six thousand people—families, dating couples, groups of children fresh out of Sunday school—passed by the bodies before a local Crown attorney found out what was going on and put a stop to things.

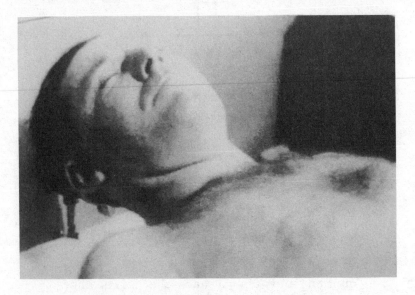

For the press, the immediate aftermath of the Sarnia shootings followed two main paths, each designed to cash in on a story that was going to sell a lot of newspapers.

First, the papers sent teams of reporters to Sarnia to interview witnesses and recreate—in print—the three minutes or so that had passed around six o'clock Saturday evening at the Christina Street liquor store. Reporters also wrote colour pieces about Constable Lewis's widow, Vera, and their two small children.

The other main thrust of the coverage involved contacting everyone responsible for Ryan's release and probing the depths of their feelings of betrayal.

R.B. Bennett

While refusing to talk to reporters himself, the former prime minister's "close friends" assured the *Star* that Mr. Bennett "felt very keenly the 'let down' occasioned by Red's reversion to crime." His friends also wanted to make something else very clear: none of this was Bennett's fault.

```
It was denied, however, that Mr.
Bennett had been responsible for
Ryan's release from the penitentiary.
Eleven years of perfect conduct won
him that through the regular parole
board channels, it was stated.
```

Senator H.A. Mullins

The best quote of them all came from the senator and cattle-man who had been so happy to tell everyone about his role in obtaining Ryan's ticket-of-leave ten months earlier. "I'm glad he is dead," Mullins told a *Star* reporter from his daughter's home in Toronto, sitting on the very terrace, we are told, where he had met Ryan shortly after the prisoner's release. "He inspired so much confidence in me that I still can't believe it. I'm done with human nature."

Unlike his comments of the previous summer, when he thought he was talking about credit, now that it was clear he was really talking about blame, the senator seemed much more willing to spread it around: "I admit starting the machinery, but Bennett finished it. We were both fooled."

His wife—who was responsible for first bringing Ryan's plight to her husband's attention after feeling "terribly sorry for him" when she saw him at Union Station back in 1924, waiting to board the train that would take him to Kingston for the rest of his life—was also in shock over the recent turn of events. "He said he'd been Christianized," Mrs. Mullins repeated several times in a low voice. "He said he was going to live right. I can't forget how he sat right here and told us."

Father Wilfred Kingsley

The *Star*'s Kingsley reaction piece was by Roy Greenaway, who writes in his memoir, *The News Game*, that he was the one who called Kingsley to break the news about Sarnia and then drove out to Kingston to interview him.

As a priest, Kingsley couldn't be treated like a politician. Culpability wasn't an option here, not that Greenaway would have played it that way anyway. No, Kingsley's role in the final chapter of the Red Ryan story would be as the victim of the ultimate betrayal.

After opening his story with Father Kingsley pleading that Greenaway not ask him any questions—"I am refusing all interviews. I don't want to discuss anything"—we are told that "with a gesture of anguish, as if trying to brush away the whole remembrance, he crushed his right hand over his eyes and cheek till the fingers whitened."

The good priest then disclosed to Greenaway "in just one exclamation" that "the devastating ingratitude of the man he had befriended cut him to the heart." It was, Greenaway wrote, "just as three centuries ago the great dramatist brooded on the fact that the winter was not so unkind as man's ingratitude." (I am a little surprised Greenaway turned to *As You Like It* in such a moment of great tragedy, particularly when Antony's "unkindest cut of all" was practically crying out to be used. I suspect he simply reached for his *Bartlett's* and looked up "ingratitude.")

Next to Kingsley's desk, thrown into a full wastepaper basket, Greenaway tells us, is a portrait of a smiling Ryan, inscribed "To my very loyal friend."

Greenaway's visit with Kingsley ends with the two men seemingly in agreement that the priest should not blame himself for the deaths that, in fact, he was more responsible for than anyone, other than Ryan: "Yet he could not blame himself. . . . The parole board, the warden, Rt. Hon. R.B. Bennett, scores of the shrewdest and most astute men in Canada, had been deceived, and had erred in judgement on the human side."

Greenaway never revised his opinion of the priest. Thirty years later, in his memoir, he called Father Kingsley "the real tragic figure" in the Ryan story. "In his eight months of freedom, Ryan was responsible for killing two men and making a third an invalid. In my books, Ryan killed another man, and that man was Father Kingsley. It was just the same as if he had fired a gun at his benefactor's head," Greenaway wrote.

I think Ryan's shot hit Kingsley in the ego, not the head. It was a bigger target anyway.

Dr. Oswald Withrow

"I am absolutely staggered."

The good doctor claimed to have known Red Ryan better than any other man, but had to admit that what he called Ryan's "Indian summer" of crime had him completely baffled. "I am something of a psychiatrist and a psychologist," he bragged to the *Star*, but, "Who could have guessed this, I give up. What's the answer?"

Struggling to come up with one, the expert in human behaviour suggested Ryan may have just been trying to help a friend. "I know he had enough money for himself," Withrow said. "There is just a chance that he wanted to help the other fellow get some."

There you go.

He also announced that Ryan's book, which he had recently finished editing, would still be published. But Ryan's ex-prison mate announced he was changing the title from "The Futility of Crime" to "The Strange Case of Red Ryan" and that he planned to write a final chapter about his friend's return to crime, his "Jekyll and Hyde character" and his death. Withrow said he was expecting "big money." But, as Frank Rasky put it so well, "no one was interested in publishing it any more."

VARIOUS OTHER BIT players in the Ryan saga were also sought out for their thoughts.

The retired police magistrate who presided over Ryan's last trial, and had been one of the first to express his support for Ryan's reformation, was asked to comment. Emerson

Coatsworth now said that he had always "felt uncertain" about Ryan's sincerity.

The former chief keeper at Kingston Penitentiary, the man Ryan had clubbed with a pitchfork during his prison break in 1923, was also asked for comment. Matt Walsh said he didn't carry a grudge against Ryan for the pitchfork incident. "In fact, I kind of liked him." But he did recall how, the last time he saw Ryan, a few weeks before his death, Red's hair had looked darker than normal. Thinking about it now, Walsh wondered if Ryan was back to his old tricks, dying his hair brown to escape detection during his "criminal robberies."

Too bad he didn't think about it then.

It should go without saying that in the course of locating and seeking comment from the cast of characters responsible for Ryan's release and the deaths of at least four men, no reporter ever considered turning to a colleague. No journalist thought to put the *Star*'s editor, Harry Hindmarsh, on the spot. Or Roy Greenaway. Or Ryan's boyhood chum, Athol Gow. It would be impossible to even imagine such a thing.

Chronicling events for a newspaper back then, or any media outlet today, creates a sense of disconnection from the events themselves. For reporters and editors, that can feel at times like a kind of purity or innocence, but the act of reporting is not a passive one. It is not pure reflection. The act of reporting affects the events themselves and the participating players, often profoundly. Sometimes that influence is premeditated, through the manipulation of facts or the torquing of emotion. Sometimes it's more accidental, simply the result of taking a story at face value when it comes from a priest, say, or a senator, and putting it in the paper to be consumed by a public unable to differentiate between information and truth.

SPEAKING OF REPORTING, that's a great lede at the top of this chapter, isn't it? Strong, short, punchy. I particularly like the dismissive "gunman and thug" and the fact that "had the life shot out of him" manages to sound both graphic and matter-of-fact at the same time.

Ledes are a particular obsession of mine, dating back to my earliest days as a newspaper reporter. My first editor would bring in copies of the *National Enquirer* and leave them lying around the office for the reporters to read, because he loved their ledes so much. He was always breaking in young reporters and he wanted us to learn how to write ledes like the *Enquirer* did, because they were so effective at hooking the reader into the story.

Reading the *Star* lede, you might ask yourself, Why not end it with the word "officers"? Isn't shorter better? Couldn't we have learned about the cops' lack of experience with guns later in the story? But that last bit is my favourite part. It's another dig. The dashing Golden Boy of Crime, whose public modesty always hinted at depths of ruthless competency, had his ass shot off by two guys who'd never fired their guns before.

Ryan's incompetence was a theme the papers and the police would return to. I suppose, having been humiliated, the urge to strike back with some humiliation of your own is very strong.

Here's how the *Star* described the actions of the two officers after Lewis had been shot: "They, with nine shots between them, destroyed both the notorious Ryan and his fellow criminal, Harry Checkley." Ryan was shot in the temple, the *Star* reported, "as he fumbled with the lock on the door leading out of the liquor store."

The *Star* quoted the Sarnia police chief talking about how proud he was of "his boys": "They stood up to one of the toughest gangsters on the continent: yes, anywhere, for that matter. They swapped shots with him, about one shot to his two, and beat him."

To the *Globe*, the chief said, "Well, my boys kept at it and they got them both. Those two fellows asked for it and they got it." The *Globe*'s reporter, Harold Dingman, who clearly knew a thing or two about holdups, added, "they bungled horribly, overlooked obvious factors necessary to a successful hold-up. Their stupidity cost them their lives."

While I think it's safe to say Ryan would have loved a lot of the coverage of his violent end, he wouldn't have cared much for this stuff.

Always looking for a fresh angle, the *Star* ran a piece in which the opinion of two psychiatrists (one anonymous) was reported. One, who had met Ryan a couple of times, diagnosed him as "abnormal, but not insane." The other, after stressing that Ryan did not have a Jekyll and Hyde type of personality, despite what Dr. Withrow would have us believe, did offer his opinion that Ryan should have never been allowed to re-enter society; he should have been locked up "like a wild beast."

———

ALMOST IMMEDIATELY, in Monday's *Globe*, which was the first paper published after the Saturday shootings (obviously there were no Toronto papers printed on Sunday), Ryan was connected to the Stonehouse killing in Markham. His brother Russ (the one who'd changed his surname) had contacted the police. By Wednesday, both the *Star* and the *Globe* were reporting that James Stonehouse (the *Globe* called him John) had identified Ed McMullen as the man who killed his father. The *Star* put McMullen's face on the front page.

Red's brother also told the police about the Quebec bank job the gang pulled just before McMullen left Toronto for the west coast, and various other successful and unsuccessful robberies and safecrackings.

McMullen, always edgy, didn't wait long to make his move. On Thursday morning he boarded a bus in Vancouver, headed for Seattle. He was carrying two pistols and seven hundred dollars in cash. At the border crossing in Blaine, Washington, U.S. immigration officials didn't believe his story that he was a railway switchman heading to Seattle to get his teeth fixed. He had no identification, for one thing. His hands didn't look like labourer's hands, for another.

When a customs officer was called in to search him, McMullen pulled out his gun and started firing. One of the bullets hit an immigration inspector in the heart, killing him. The customs officer who was about to conduct the search, Leroy J. Pike, wrapped his arms around McMullen from behind. McMullen angled his gun up over his shoulder, trying to shoot Pike in the face, but just as he pulled the trigger, the customs officer managed to deflect the pistol. Wyoming

McMullen shot himself in the head. He lingered in hospital a couple of days before dying.

McMullen's capture and death received plenty of coverage in the Toronto papers because of his connection to Ryan. One story called him a "lieutenant" in the Red Ryan gang, but according to a former deputy warden at the Kingston Pen, who had retired in Vancouver and was interviewed there while McMullen was dying in a Seattle hospital, it probably should have been called the McMullen gang. R.R. Tucker, the man who had called McMullen "the most dangerous man I ever knew in Kingston," said he believed Ryan was the follower, not the leader.

```
Ryan was volatile, easily led.
McMullen was cold as ice, silent,
immovable as a Gypsy's curse. Ryan
had a bright future when he left
penitentiary. McMullen had none but
crime. I have no doubt he lured Ryan
away from the path of rectitude.
```

Maybe Wyoming McMullen, who apparently always hated the nickname that Ernest Hemingway gave him, would have preferred being called the Gypsy's Curse. In any event, despite what Tucker said, I don't think Ryan needed much in the way of luring.

Is THIS A good time to catch up with the rest of the boys who went up and over the wall at Kingston back in 1923? In case you've forgotten, they were, as Hemingway described them: Big Simpson, the "husky" with the heavy under-shot jaw; Young Brown, the "slim kid" with the cap pulled over his eyes; Runty Bryans, the "little runt" who scrambled like a monkey; the "thick set, ham-faced" Wyoming McMullen; and Red Ryan, the freckle-faced man with the "flaming head."

You've just read about Red and the ham-faced Ed McMullen. Young Brown—a.k.a. Arthur Brown, a.k.a. Andrew Sullivan, a.k.a. Curly Sullivan, a.k.a. Peanut-head Sullivan— you also know about: shot through the heart by police as he stood in the doorway of his girlfriend's flat in Minneapolis.

But what happened to Runty?

I know it's not very professional to admit this, but Runty was always my favourite. All the shots of him that I've seen are of the "mug" variety, but at least in this one his hair is combed, his eyes are relatively clear, and he's somehow managed to come into the possession of a nice, pressed three-piece suit.

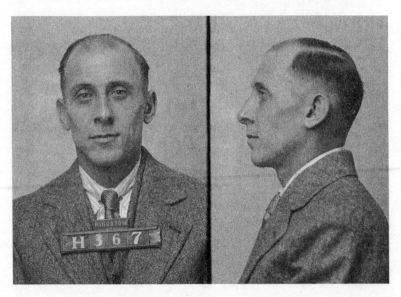

Somewhere in the piles of photocopied newspaper and magazine articles, old books and printouts from websites with names like the Sarnia Historical Society and Toronto Wrestling History, which cover both levels of my desk, the chair next to my desk and a portion of the floor around my desk, is a description of Runty Bryans as being remarkably strong. All I've got to do is find it.

(I really have to work on my data retrieval system. I'm starting to think that marking items of interest with a yellow highlighter begins to lose its effectiveness after a couple of hundred paragraphs have been highlighted.)

No, I spoke too soon. I found it. The system works.

It was in the *Star*, in the first wave of Sarnia coverage, in the middle of a long recap of Ryan's criminal career. Writing about the prison break, the story lists the men who escaped with Ryan, ending with "and Thomas 'Runty' Bryans, a short man of exceptional physical strength."

This is the only reference I've come across to Runty's strength, and I have to say I have my doubts. The man had two nicknames. His newspaper nickname, thanks to the author of *For Whom the Bell Tolls*, was Runty. His walking-around nickname was Shorty. If he was so strong, why did he let people call him Runty and Shorty?

Surprisingly, he was the last of the cons to be caught after the Kingston escape. He was picked up in Chicago in March 1927, after claiming a man had stolen twenty dollars from him in a saloon. Unfortunately for Runty, the saloonkeeper called the police. When Runty told the cops he wanted to drop the matter, they became suspicious. It didn't take long for them to find Runty's picture in their files. But he had managed to evade capture for about three and a half years before being sent back to Kingston.

You just knew that things were not going to end well for the Runt. The headline on the front page of the February 7, 1938, edition of the now-amalgamated *Globe and Mail* read "Toronto Murder Laid to One of Ryan Gang." Red Ryan could still sell papers, almost two years after his death.

Under it is a depressing story.

> Thomas (Shorty) Bryans, one of the notorious Red Ryan gang, was taken in custody early Sunday morning on a charge of murder a few minutes after Norman Ford . . . was slain in the shadow of Keele Street Police Station.
>
> Bryans, also known as "Bunty," was trapped by Police Sergeant Earl Scott after a brief chase. The small, shabbily-dressed man pulled his gun out as the policeman closed in on him. He pulled the trigger. Nothing happened. The gun jammed.
>
> Scott grabbed Bryans and swung his ham-like fist with a crack to the jaw of the Ryan gangster. . . . Bryans fell flat on his face.

A few things to point out here. First, notice the three short sentences that end the second paragraph and the use of "ham" as a descriptor in paragraph three. I think the *Globe* may have had a Hemingway fan on staff. I wonder if Runty, seeing Sergeant Scott's fist heading his way, noted a resemblance to Ed McMullen's face.

Also, this is the newspaper article where "Runty" was misspelled "Bunty," something I have remarked on before.

You'll note that if he was endowed with exceptional physical strength, it apparently slipped his mind in all the excitement.

And finally, notice the repeated references to Bryans's membership in the Ryan gang, which would continue in the press coverage of his trial. Runty Bryans contrived somehow to be included in the group of men who went over the wall at Kingston, but was never a member of the Ryan gang. He wasn't a bank robber. He was a drunk and, in Peter McSherry's memorable phrase, "a career mugger."

On the night of the Ford killing, when questioned by police, Bryans's only remark was, "I don't know anything about a shooting. I'm drunk." Bryans and Ford had met only that night. They had been drinking together and had been seen "walking arm and arm" about half an hour before the shooting. Bryans had tried to rob Ford and Ford had resisted, so Bryans shot him.

Thomas "Runty" Bryans, "the last of the Red Ryan Gang," as he was known in the papers, was hanged in Toronto's Don Jail five months later.

But how could Runty be "the last of the Red Ryan Gang" when Big Simpson was still kicking around?

Gordon Simpson didn't manage to stay free after the escape for as long as Runty Bryans, but he did quite a bit better than McMullen, Sullivan and Ryan. After splitting up from the rest of the escapees, Simpson made his way to the States, where he worked in construction and on the railroads. He enlisted as a seaman and eventually made his way to Germany, where he lived under the name of Hall.

He decided to return to the United States and was arrested as he stepped off the S.S. *America* at the Hudson Terminal Building in New York City in November 1925, turned in for the reward money by a fellow ex-con whom he had befriended. He had been free for over two years.

But here's the thing: Simpson returned to Kingston, served his time and then went straight. According to the best information Peter McSherry was able to find, Big Simpson lived in Quebec until he died sometime in the late 1970s, making him, by a substantial margin, the last of the Ryan gang.

ANOTHER THEME of a bunch of the post-Sarnia coverage was speculation about the impact Ryan's fall would have on the country's parole system. And it certainly did have an impact. In an article written for *Maclean's* magazine over twenty years after Ryan's death, the writer Ted Honderich quoted the director of Ontario's probation services as saying that Ryan's case had set back the progress of parole in Canada by fifteen years. "That one spectacular case did more against the system than the proven record of thousands of men has done for it," D.W.F. Coughlin said.

Honderich himself called the Ryan story "a tragicomedy that left Canada with one of the most backward parole systems in the western world."

Not bad for the guy who said, right after his release, that his deepest concern was doing anything that would jeopardize the chances of other inmates being given the second chance he had received.

But all this is parenthetical to the final story of the man himself. His last journey was a short one. Shot dead on Saturday. Put on public display Sunday. Picked up by his brother and brought to Toronto by train on Monday.

On the afternoon of Tuesday, May 26, 1936, a small crowd of four or five people, including Ryan's brother and Jack Corcoran, the wrestling promoter who'd given him a job, watched as Red Ryan's coffin was lowered into unconsecrated ground, the archbishop having denied him the last rites of the Roman Catholic Church. It was a decision that, presumably, continues to have major implications for the eternal soul of Norman J. Ryan.

When Red Ryan killed Constable John Lewis of the Sarnia police force, he shot him four times with his revolver at point-blank range, from no more than four or five feet away. But here's a strange truth: only one of the bullets injured Lewis. According to the autopsy that was performed the night of the shooting, one of the bullets hit a large brass button on the front of Lewis's tunic and was deflected away. Two other bullets were deflected by a small book of fish and game laws Lewis was carrying in his tunic's breast pocket. Only one bullet entered Lewis's body, "drilled through the centre of the officer's chest," as the *Globe* reported.

Obviously, one bullet was enough, but it's remarkable how close he came to walking away from four shots fired point-blank into his chest.

GUN BATTLE IN SARNIA ENDS LIFE OF RED RYAN AND COMPANION

Upper left, exterior of [r]ight occurred; upper right, interior of store where twenty-five customers were lined up; lower left, guns used by Ryan to kill young Sarnia policeman; centre, clever device of mirror (arrow) used by bandits for rear vision; lower right, guns used by [...] identified. Ph[...]

s Reject Proposals

Tory Leadership Aspirants Will Await Election Decision

CLAIMING the wiser course to pursue would be to secure a repeal of the Hepburn Government's corporation tax legislation first, candidates for the leadership of the Conservative Party have turned down a demand from members of the Orange Order that they should agree to submit to the courts for a decision all "concessions" given to Roman Catholics and Separate Schools since 1863.

Fear Public Opinion.

The Globe was informed on Saturday that at least one candidate for the leadership of the party had taken the stand that a move to wipe out all "concessions" of which there are [w]ould turn public opinion against the party.

Members of the order who have discussed a general attack on the separate schools have been advised that their proposals can be dealt with after the corporation tax legislation has been disposed of through a general election.

If a pro-Protestant Leader and the Conservative Party is successful in a general election, it is suspected, another move on the part of the Orange [...]

EXPLOSIVES FOUND NEAR RYAN HOUSE

Search of Garage in Toronto Reveals Quantity of Dynamite

On learning of the death of Norman Ryan, the Toronto police immediately joined in the police investigation.

Gaining an entrance to Ryan's garage in the rear of Lansdowne Avenue, Detective-Sergeant Thomas Whitelaw and Detective Lister Sullivan seized a black suitcase containing 9 sticks of dynamite, a 26-ounce bottle of nitro-glycerine, 5 glass sealers containing fuses and caps.

This was similar, the police said, to what was found in the stolen car found near the scene of the murder of Constable Lewis in Sarnia.

The garage search followed a search of Ryan's room during the early morning hours by Detective-Sergeant William McAllister and Detective J. Nimmo. The police stated nothing incriminating was found in Ryan's room.

When Whitelaw and Sullivan made their way into the garage Ryan's own car was parked there. Nothing was in it. They then walked over to a corner of the garage. Whitelaw lifted an old overcoat. Beneath it was the black leather handbag. On opening the police found the explosives. These were taken to police headquarters.

LIQUOR STORES

Ryan [...] "Fu[...]

Dr. Withrow, as [...] Adviser, S[...] Violent De[...] Convict

I am absolu[...] [...]ed," said [...] Withrow, w[...]

Ryan in priso[...] was told of the [...] friend before [...] the Sarnia poli[...]

Edited Ryan's Book[...]

Dr. Withrow, as surgeon at Kingston[...] close to the life [...] of Ryan, and it w[...] that the ex-convict cently completed b[...] of Crime." Dr. [...] Ryan and the asse[...] he led at Kingston[...]

Dr. Withrow has [...] ing the autobiogra[...] to the story of a [...] added a conclusion written by Ryan [...]

"It was only si[...] we were discussing [...] office," said Dr W[...] to be sure, Red, I [...] time. Have you th[...] tion or desire for [...] "Absolutely none[...] reply.

The doctor stated[...] the time Ryan w[...] Kingston: "I can[...] that Red will make [...] a chance."

Police Were Fair.

es Boo
of Cri

Ryan Had Gold
tunity to Re
Former King
lain

NEVER was
vict given s
opportunity
the wreckage o
past," was outsta
statement made
Globe yesterday
Rev. Father King
r chaplain at
enitentiary an
dviser to Norn
Ryan during his
riest concluded
g to abandonme
y other criminal
enerous treatme
aw might some
or them.

ought Reform Comp
The statement, in fu
The despatch from
public with a sense
disappointment. Ne
vict given such gold
rebuild the wreckag
and effectively as
ciates in rebuilding
rded Norman ("Red
even the highest

CHAPTER
15

LITTLE RED
LIES

15

The documentary filmmaker Errol Morris describes history as "perishable": "it has an expiration date. It's like food left in the refrigerator too long. Records are lost, people die, evidence is corrupted, manipulated, and it becomes increasingly hard to go back to the actual events." For Morris, this is a problem. In his films, he sees himself as an investigator on the trail of the truth, so history's perishability makes his work more difficult. For me, though, with this project, the prospect of poking at a piece of turned fruit or mouldy cheese forgotten in the back of the fridge excites me at least as much as coming across an unspoiled, pure fact.

So, yes, we can look at this life of Ryan as an attempt to separate the facts from the myths. But can we also agree that the myths must remain? Can we agree together to love the lies?

Red Ryan's entire life was, in all the important details anyway, an almost total fabrication. But there are some small pieces of delightful shit-crockery associated with the Ryan myth that I'd like to extract from the larger, heaping pile and spend some time with.

Let's start with my personal favourite, Ryan the Genius Inventor. In November 1926, it was reported on the front page of the *Globe* that Red Ryan, who had been working in Kingston's mailbag department, had invented a thief-proof lock for mailbags that had been adopted by the postal service. The lock was so well designed, the *Globe* claimed, that even Red himself couldn't pick it.

Seven years later, in his *Star Weekly* piece on Father Kingsley, Roy Greenaway picked up on the story.

> The logical mind of Ryan found another outlet. In 1927 the Scientific American reported him as an inventor. In his spare time he had invented a new mail-bag lock. "This is something out of the ordinary in the way of a locking device," was the official verdict of the chief industrial officer of the penitentiary transmitted to Ottawa. And he added: "My candid opinion is that it is far superior to any locking device the

post office is using to-day." Besides its
other qualifications it was thief proof.

Many stories followed over the years, suggesting Ryan's relatives were living well off the royalties from the lock, and it became a standard feature of the Ryan myth that his unpickable lock was in use with the postal service. Thirty years after Ryan's death, in his memoirs, Greenaway was still polishing the old story up, although somehow the name of the magazine he cited had changed: "In 1926 he invented a thief-proof mail bag, which was cited by *Popular Science Monthly* and put into use by Canadian postal authorities."

As stories go, this one was very sticky. It was also a lie, and a lie that had been publicly exposed years earlier in the pages of the *Star*, had Greenaway been interested in learning the truth. Looking into the allegations that Ryan's heirs were living high off the hog on the proceeds from the lock, *Star* reporters found that, while Ryan had applied for a patent for his lock, it had expired years earlier. A post office spokesperson told the *Star* that Ryan's lock had been considered for use, but rejected, apparently after it was discovered it could be easily picked with a nail. So was that the real story? Had Ryan invented a mailbag lock that didn't work? Maybe not.

In 1981, Peter McSherry interviewed a former guard who had worked in the mailbag department in 1926, and he told McSherry that Wyoming McMullen had invented the lock, with Ryan's help. "I watched them do it," Oren Earl said. McSherry figures it was Father Kingsley who tipped off the *Globe* for the original story. It was certainly Kingsley who told Greenaway about it. Which means the myth of Ryan the Genius Inventor was likely based on lies told by a priest.

The next tall tale is tougher to trace to its roots. Since it doesn't really redound to Ryan's credit, I don't think we can blame it on him or any of his ghostwriters. It just sort of sits there, adding a very nice dash of irony to the end of his story.

If you poke around online looking for references to Red Ryan, one tidbit of information invariably turns up. For example, this is from an article about Ryan and the death of Constable John Lewis on the website of the Sarnia Historical Society. The writer is referring to Ryan's return to Toronto after his release from Kingston in 1935: "Job offers flooded in, and he was even given his own show on radio station CFRB, where he continued to lament the waste that was a life of crime." This is from a blog written by a federal inmate serving time for murder, which used to appear regularly on the *Vancouver Sun* website:

> *By 1935, he was back in the mix, this time hosting a popular radio show on Toronto's CFRB. Part Coach's Corner, part old-time religion. . . .*
>
> *Police legend has it that Red's daily transmission was just winding down at the same time robbery squad detectives were peeling the gore-soaked mask from his lifeless face.*

And this is from Ryan's Wikipedia page:

> *After his release he hosted a popular radio program on CFRB where he denounced the criminal lifestyle and his own past life. . . .*

The last broadcast of Ryan's programme on CFRB came directly before the news broadcast about his death in Sarnia.

The reference Wikipedia cites to back up this claim is a feature story called "Once upon a City," published in November 2016 in the *Toronto Star*. Here is what that article says:

> After his release he sold cars at a dealership, denounced crime on the CFRB radio show he'd been given and wrote (with the help of a ghost writer), "crime doesn't pay" articles for the Star. . . .
>
> Ironically, the last broadcast of Ryan's radio program came just before the news announcement of his shoot-out death.

So, in other words, this:

INTERIOR: LIVING ROOM: EVENING, MAY 1936

Three young children are sitting on a living room rug in front of a large floor model radio. They are listening raptly to their favourite program.

VOICE ON RADIO: So, boys and girls, remember what your old pal Red Ryan told you: listen to your parents and teachers, and, like I always say, crime doesn't —
NEW VOICE ON RADIO: We interrupt this program to bring you this breaking news story from Sarnia, Ontario . . .

CUT TO:

The faces of the children, reacting with growing shock as the news sinks in.

It's a great story, but I don't buy it.

Peter McSherry, who spent over twenty years research-ing Ryan and was a CFRB listener, never mentioned it in his book. Neither did Martin Robin, who did some research, and Frank Rasky, who didn't. Neither Roy Greenaway nor Jocko Thomas, the *Star* reporter who took Red along when he was sent to cover a fire, mentioned it in their memoirs. Since both journalists were around at the time, and both would have loved adding that extra bit of colour to their yarns, it seems like a strange omission. Even more so for Thomas, who was a regu-lar on CFRB for years before his retirement in the late 1980s.

There's also the fact that nowhere in the extensive news-paper coverage of Ryan's death is there any mention of his radio program, much less the fact that the last episode aired right before the news of the Sarnia shooting was broadcast.

CFRB, which now goes by the name NEWSTALK 1010, has no information about it, or any archive recordings of Red Ryan, but that isn't surprising for a radio station. Up until the digital era, almost nothing that went out over the airwaves was archived. Library and Archives Canada has plenty of CFRB recordings from the year in question, but none featuring Red Ryan. Almost all of them deal with the abdication of King Edward VIII.

So where did this story come from? And how did Canada's largest newspaper come to report it?

I tried to reach the author of the *Star* piece, by both phone and email, to find out where she got her information, with no luck. So I can only surmise what happened. I know that the CFRB program was mentioned in Ryan's Wikipedia bio before the *Star* piece was written. If you check the history of the page, CFRB appears to have been in the original version posted in 2009, while the *Star* article didn't appear until 2016.

So here's what I think. The *Star* writer saw the story on Wikipedia and included it in her historical feature, which was a light piece anyway, so why spend too much time fact-checking? A Wikipedia editor saw the *Star* piece, and tagged it on Ryan's Wikipedia page as a reference, proving the truth of the Wikipedia story that was the *Star* writer's source. Where Wikipedia originally got it from is anybody's guess, but now everyone, from bloggers to historical society contributors, can write about it, secure in the cover given them by the great journalistic resources of the *Toronto Star*.

If I'm right, journalism hasn't changed much over the past eighty years.

Or perhaps this story is bigger than that. Bigger even than our notions about truth and lies. Perhaps myths just simply need that last ironic twist, and the physics of the thing take over where a vacuum exists. Needless to say, that scene with the children seated in front of the radio is going in the movie. As the occasional film producer and noted hermit Howard Hughes once said, "Never check an interesting fact."

RYAN'S JEKYLL AND HYDE CAREER EXPOSED IN SARNIA DEATH DUEL

Held up as a splendid example of the reformed convict and to all appearances justifying the faith of many prominent people who took a keen interest in him, Norman "Red" Ryan of Toronto had his Jekyll and Hyde existence exposed Saturday night at Sarnia when he was shot dead in an attempted hold-up of a liquor store after he killed Constable Jack Lewis of the Sarnia police force. A striking portrait of Ryan (2) by the Gainsboro studio, taken last Christmas, contrasts sharply with Harry Checkley (3), hardened criminal, who accompanied Ryan in the fateful Sarnia attempted hold-up and like Ryan fell mortally wounded from police bullets. The children of the slain Sarnia police officer, Jack Lewis, are shown in (1). Donna, 10, is holding "Speck," their pet dog, with her brother, Jack Jr., 8, at her side. (4) Clothing and license plates found in Ryan's car. The letter on the license plate was originally an E but had been altered to pass for an F at a few feet. (5) Ryan's .45 calibre black automatic from which all eleven bullets had been discharged and his .38 calibre Ivor Johnson revolver. (6) Sergt. Geo. Smith, who along with Det. Frank McGirr, followed Constable Lewis into the liquor store and after Lewis was shot to death engaged Ryan and Checkley in a gun duel, fatally wounding them. (7) Constable Jack Lewis, one of the most popular officers on the Sarnia force, who was shot down and killed by Ryan when they met face to face in the liquor store. (8) Fuses, detonator caps and dynamite and the box in which they were found in Ryan's car. (9) Detective Frank McGirr, who along with Sergt. Smith shot down Ryan and his companion. (10) Constable Lewis' modest home on Nelson St., Sarnia. (11) Motorcycle Officer Simpkins, who stood on guard outside the liquor store after he found the entrance door locked.

...BNORMAL BUT NOT INSANE SAYS PSYCHIATRIST OF RYAN

...ject to Certain Urges, Dr. ...McGhie Thinks—Doubt Dual Nature

...EDED EXCITEMENT

...ange and interesting case for ...chiatrists, Norman Ryan, in the ...ion of Dr. B. T. McGhie, dep... minister of health for Ontario ...an outstanding mental expert, ...ld not be classified as insane. ..."I have met him and talked to ... briefly on a few occasions," ... McGhie stated to-day, when ...ed for his diagnosis.

"The only definition of insanity ...have is section 19 of the code. ...certain he didn't come under ...section that defines an insane ...son as one who does not know ...nature and effect of his actions. ...sure Ryan did, from my conver...ons with him.

"It is obvious now from his his...y that he was of abnormal per...ality and make-up, and was sub... to certain urges, but that is a ...ferent thing from insanity, al...ugh it is sometimes called that ...the United States. I think we're ...agreed that there was something ...ormal about Ryan. I suppose ...d fit into the group we call ...chopathic personalities."

Although recognizing Ryan's ex...sive egotism and visualization of ...nself as a centre of collective in...st, Dr. McGhie did not consider ...s as a serious symptom.

"He met so many people not in ...normal walk of life who made ...te a fuss about him under the ...cumstances that he did exactly ...at a lot of people would have ...ne who were patted like that on ...e back."

Not Dual Personality

Although the average person is ...mpted to think of Ryan as a sort ...dual personality, like Robt. Louis ...evenson's Dr. Jekyll and Mr. Hyde, ... outstanding psychiatrist, who ...ished to remain anonymous, em...hasized Ryan did not fit this cate...ory.

"A dual personality does happen ...ometimes," he said. "A dual per...onality is one that is completely ...plit, so that the one part doesn't ...now what the other does. But ...yan was not in that category. He ...ist led a respectable life on the ...rface, and calculated to exploit it ...r the purpose of acumulating ...ealth quickly in a hidden, illegal ...ay.

"There is no doubt that Ryan ...eded to get the feeling of excite...ent and power he got in these ...old-ups.

Like Wild Beast, Is View

"The terrible thing is that, with ...s perfectly recognizable abnor...ality, they would let him out, ...en he should be kept away from ...ciety like a wild beast. This con...tion of Ryan's could be recognized ...sily. At most, I should think one ...ld be certain of it in a three or

THIRTY INJURED WEEK-END TOLL

Toronto's traffic toll over the week-end:

Dead	0
Injured	30
Toronto's toll for the year:	
Dead	16
Injured	1,123

ONTARIO PAROLE BD. DIDN'T RELEASE RYAN

Machinery Set Up by Federal Government Responsible for His Freedom

By R. W. LIPSETT

Ottawa, May 26.—The machinery set up by the federal government was solely responsible for the release of Norman "Red" Ryan on ticket of leave last July.

The Ontario parole board, headed by Judge J. F. McKinley of Ottawa, had nothing to do with it, the judge pointed out emphatically to-day. The Ontario board deals only with prisoners in provincial institutions.

Under the federal system, department of justice officers, including the penitentiary branch, perform the functions of a parole board. The personnel varies somewhat, but none of these usually concerned with remission of sentences would say to-day that Rt. Hon. R. B. Bennett, then prime minister, had intervened to secure or hasten Ryan's release.

It was admitted to be generally understood that Mr. Bennett was interested in Ryan and it was known that he spent almost an hour in conversation with him during a visit to Kingston penitentiary, but there is no record that he asked for his release.

The first definite point in the move toward consideration of ticket-of-leave for Ryan came following the 1933 riots in the penitentiary, the warden's report crediting Ryan with an important part in helping quell them. Then followed reports of his model conduct during the ten years after his sentence to life for the Hamilton hold-up. Prison inspectors and superintendents checked up and a very laudatory file on behalf of Ryan was built up in the office of the remission branch.

It was about this time that Ryan's case came into wide attention through his interview with Mr. Bennett, and rumors that he was to be released were prevalent. It was several months, however, before the department of justice took definite action and Ryan walked out from the prison.

ADMITTED STEAIING GUNS

Conviction of Elgin Robinson Sus-

MEN'S POLICE COURT

ON WAY TO 'BIG HOUSE' CROWN WARNS YOUTH

Gets Six Months for Receiving Stolen Watch — Says Juvenile Gave It to Him

Convicted of receiving a stolen watch, Frank Smokler was sentenced to six months in jail by Magistrate Jones in No. 2 men's court.

Det. John O'Driscoll testified that a juvenile was charged with theft. The watch was stolen from the home of Joseph Bain, the officer said.

Smokler was apprehended after the juvenile was arrested, witness continued.

Smokler stated the juvenile had given him the watch, saying he had found it. "Why didn't you report it to the police? You must have known something was wrong, an 11-year-old boy giving in a watch," said Magistrate Jones. "My mother can tell you that is right," said accused. "You ought to be ashamed of yourself, bringing in your mother like that. You should have known better," said the magistrate.

"Where did you get the new car you have been driving around?" asked Mr. Malone. "I was working at selling rugs for a while," replied Smokler.

"I have a suspicion you told the boy who gave you the watch where he could get the watch," said Mr. Malone. "No, sir," said Smokler.

"You haven't turned Fagin yet then," declared Mr. Malone. "You've

14 days in jail, dating back to May 15.

Has to Pay Costs

At the request of the complainant, Victor Binder, charges of theft and aggravated assault were withdrawn against Jack Goldbar. "If you are withdrawing the charges you will have to pay the costs," said the magistrate. Binder had some anxious moments when he discovered he did not have the $10 required. A court officer was leading him from the court, when Goldbar's counsel came to his rescue with a $10 bill.

Siphon Was Too Short

"I didn't have any money and I wanted to go to a dance in Long Branch. I couldn't have gone anyway because the officer tells me that the hose was too short and I could not have siphoned any of the gasoline," declared Harry Sidney, pleading guilty of attempted theft of gasoline from an automobile. The officer said he caught Sidney in the act of siphoning the gasoline from the tank of another automobile.

Learning it was accused's first *offence of any kind*, the magistrate remanded him for sentence.

Sorry Accused Studying Law

"I hope you have changed your attitude about this case. I am shocked to hear you are thinking of becoming a lawyer. I don't think anyone with your idea of thinking you have the right to shoot a six-year-old boy in the eye because he wouldn't listen to you, would be a credit to our profession. It would be lamentable if you ever became a lawyer, you would be giving your clients the same idea. I hope you are stopped in time," declared Magistrate Jones as Sydney Blackman appeared for sentence for wounding a six-year-old boy by hitting him in the eye with a pellet from an air-rifle when the lad refused to leave Blackman's yard. "Did you like studying in jail?" asked Mr. Jones. Blackburn didn't reply.

He was fined $25 and costs or one month.

$25 and 14 Days For Taking Bets

Pleading guilty of registering and recording bets on horse races, George Baker was fined $25 and costs or 10 days and 14 days in jail. Baker stated this was the only way he could keep off relief, as he had not been working for four years. He was making about $20 a day, he said.

Morgan Ritchie pleaded guilty of theft of five yards of sod from the city. "I didn't steal it. It was on my truck and then I put it back," he said at first. "Where would it have been if the officer had not seen you?" asked Mr. Malone. "In my back yard to finish off a nice job," replied Ritchie. "I guess I'm guilty," he added. He was remanded for sentence on his promise he would not do it again.

Ryan Had Enough Nitro To Blow Up Half of City

Enough dynamite and nitroglycerine to blow up "half of Toronto," according to the police, was found Sunday morning in a garage—rented by Norman J. "Red" Ryan—in a laneway that runs between Lansdowne Ave. and St. Helens Ave., south of Dundas W.

It was found by Ryan's brother, who came within an ace of running over a small black brief bag hidden beneath an old overcoat. The brother had been left Ryan's small roadster Saturday to use in the city and it was while backing the car into Ryan's own garage that the rear wheels squeezed against a gasoline can at the rear and stopped Ryan's brother from backing the car any further into the garage.

Had the auto run over the dynamite or nitro-glycerine, police state

Detective Sergeant Tom Whitelaw and Detective Lister Sullivan were rushed to the garage where they took charge of the explosives.

"I suspect it is nitro-glycerine" stated Detective Whitelaw, who with Sergeant of Detectives John Hicks have been for months specializing in safe breaking gangs. "The dynamite is boiled down and the 'soup' is creamed off. These coils found in the garage are identical with the ones found at the Metropolitan store job where the safe was blasted and $2,000 stolen.

"The cords are also the same type found at the Ontario Produce Co., Market St., where the safe was all soaped and taped and the nitro sealed up in a rubber glove that had been inserted in a bored hole at the top of the door of the safe.

ERIN HORSE SHOW HELD BIG SUCCESS

Erin, May 26.—The Erin Agricultural Society presented its fifty-ninth spring horse show yesterday, with the largest attendance on record. All classes were well filled and old-timers stated that the animals on exhibition were the best ever to appear here. Mrs. R. M. Bar-

BIG CROWD ATT... BOY SCOUT JA...

70th Troop of ... Awarded First ... Neat Camp-...

Milton, May 26.—T... Ontario boy scout jam... here yesterday after ... session. Over 350 ... rovers, sea scouts ar... registered from points ... Port Dalhousie, Tro... ronto, Mimico, New ... Dennis, Weston, Oakvi... Galt, Port Credit, Act... housie and Hardingto...

The 70th Troop, ... awarded first prize f... camp-site with Port ... close second.

Saturday night the ... ceded by the George... band, paraded throug... then gathered aroun... in the centre of the c... sented a stunt progra...

Early Sunday morn... two from each troop, ... a cross-country hike ... each member being ... draw an accurate ma... taken. The 70th T... again took first priz... of 11 points out of ... The 90th Troop, Toro... while Milton was th...

Sunday afternoon ... paraded from the cam... St. Paul's United chu... colors were dedicate... A. B. Irwin of St. ... Canon L. J. R. N... Anglican church.

Port Credit sea s... prize for the neates... the Monday mornin... John C. Hall, assista... missioner of Toront...

Following the ... sports was held und... of E. Logan Willar... crew leader.

The 70th Troop, T... town of Milton shie... points, a total of 77. ... Toronto, was secon... while Mimico was t... of 56 points.

IDENTIFIES M... EVADING ...

London, Ont., Ma... a tentative identi... on, police concentr... clearing up the m... held under guard ... pital while he rec... effects of a bullet ...

Late last night, ... from headquarters ... had identified the ... McArthur, 41, ... Thomas, who latel... in Toronto and ... wounded man, ho... confirm the ident...

According to po... shot when he att... arrest after being ... downtown service ... urday.

SEEK HIT-RU... WHO INJUR...

CHAPTER 16

HINDMARSH

16

One of the very first episodes of the Canadian TV quiz show *Front Page Challenge* featured the story of Red Ryan's death in Sarnia. For those of you too young to remember, *Front Page Challenge* was kind of a cross between *To Tell the Truth* and *What's My Line*, with a dash of current affairs thrown in. Of course, if you're too young to remember *Front Page Challenge*, comparing it to *To Tell the Truth* and *What's My Line* probably doesn't help very much. Let's just say it was a national institution that first went on the air in 1957 and continued entertaining elderly Canadians until the mid-1990s.

Here's how the show worked. Four panellists, all well-known journalists, were seated facing away from a guest who had a connection to a major news story. Asking a series of yes-or-no questions—Is this a good-news story? Did this happen within the past year?—the panellists competed against each other to be the first to guess the headline.

The most famous panellist was a man named Gordon Sinclair, who began his career at the *Toronto Star*, where, the legend says, he didn't get a byline for seven years, but hung in anyway and eventually became the most popular newspaper reporter in Canada.

When Red Ryan earned his ticket-of-leave from Kingston in July 1935, Sinclair's *Star* career was at its peak. He was the paper's globetrotting star, filing reports from exotic locations all around the world. The week that Ryan was released, stories about the Golden Boy of Crime fought for front-page attention with a series of pieces Sinclair was filing from northern India. Here's a taste of Sinclair's style:

> *Srinagar, Kashmir*—The main line of the main town in Kashmir is the fast flowing Jhelum river, snow-fed from the mighty Himalayas, lined by the most rickety yet picturesque houses, schools, shops and mosques in Central Asia and peopled by velvety-eyed women and predatory salesmen who defeat their own ends by whining over and over like a cracked record: "No need to buy, your honor—just geef a look."

The combination of exotic glamour and casual racism was like catnip for readers. They couldn't get enough of his stuff. The first printing of his first book of collected travel pieces reportedly sold out in one day.

Before setting off on one of his adventures, the *Star* would hold a public farewell for Sinclair. The gathering held to say goodbye to him in 1933, before he took off for a tour of Southeast Asia, filled Toronto's Massey Hall, with—according to the *Star*—an estimated sixty-five hundred people turned away at the door. His *Star* pieces from that trip were collected in a book called *Cannibal Quest*. Here's young Gord, about to head off up the Khyber, or some such place.

Now, it must be said that not everyone believed everything Sinclair wrote in his dispatches from abroad. His series of stories from Afghanistan, for example, was so widely questioned by readers that the *Star* assigned another reporter to verify Sinclair's claims.

After being fired and rehired by the *Star* numerous times over the years for various crimes and misdemeanours (apparently, he was fired one time for failing to notice a war had broken out while he was in Ethiopia), one of the firings stuck and Sinclair left the paper. He started working for CFRB and quickly went from being the country's most popular newspaperman to being its most popular broadcaster.

Of course, as a child in the sixties and early seventies, bored to tears watching *Front Page Challenge* at my grandparents' house, I knew none of this. I didn't know anything about the dashing, young, globetrotting reporter. I just saw a cantankerous old man with a bad comb-over.

The Red Ryan episode happened well before my days as a viewer. That particular program aired sometime in late 1957 and, as far as I can determine, no copies survive. CBC Archives doesn't have a copy. There's nothing online. So we must turn to the always reliable memory of Ryan biographer Peter McSherry. Here's how he remembers it:

> *The guest was George Smith (one of the Sarnia police officers who killed Ryan); panelist Gordon Sinclair guessed the headline virtually immediately; and the program degenerated into remembrances of Ryan, principally Sinclair's. "Red Ryan was nothing but a dangerous little punk," declared Sinclair, who had been a* Toronto Star *reporter in the thirties, in characteristically direct fashion. "He was no big-time crook." Sinclair also stated that "the* Star *made Red Ryan" and "the* Star *got Ryan out of prison." When asked, "Who at the* Star*?", Sinclair answered, "Harry Hindmarsh."*

Harry Hindmarsh, or H.C.H. (his middle name was Comfort), was pretty clearly the principal author of the Red

Ryan story, even though he didn't personally write a word. He was the teetotalling managing editor of the *Star,* and ran the paper's newsroom for most of the first half of the twentieth century. He was married to the proprietor's daughter, and therefore unfireable. And he was the creator and sole implementer of what came to be called the Hindmarsh treatment, a method of driving reporters so unrelentingly that only two possible end points could be reached: complete submission to the boss, or unemployment. Actually there was a third possible end point, arrived at quite often, in fact—alcoholism.

Let's start with a physical description. According to Roy Greenaway, Hindmarsh was six feet three inches tall and weighed 220 pounds, which, in the world of the tiny men who peopled Toronto a hundred or so years ago, would have made him a giant. Hemingway biographer William Burrill describes him as "a brusque, beefy man of six foot two with a short military haircut and a stiff military bearing. He did not expect his reporters and editors to like him—in fact, he knew that most were scared stiff of him—but he did expect them to obey him without question." According to George McCullagh, the owner of the rival *Toronto Telegram,* Hindmarsh was "so ugly that if he ever bit himself, he'd get hydrophobia."

Journalist and author Pierre Berton, Gordon Sinclair's long-time co-panellist on *Front Page Challenge,* wrote a feature article about Hindmarsh for *Maclean's* magazine in 1952. Here's how he described the man:

In his 42 years at the Star, *in which he has risen from cub reporter to president, Harry Hindmarsh has neither*

answered his critics, nor coddled his admirers. His detach-
ment is such that he has never publicly displayed any of
those passions of hate, love, anger, frustration, reverence
and awe which he has inspired in others, and on which the
Star has thrived for half a century.

Greenaway spent almost his entire lengthy career working under Hindmarsh, and he clearly worshipped the man. Here's his description of Hindmarsh, under pressure:

An aura of immobility and command seemed to surround
him. Even in moments of crisis his calmness never deserted
him. Coming out of his redoubt when a hot story was
breaking, he was the Supreme Commander on the floor
of the editorial room. In his deep, slow voice, he issued his
instructions to his troops, speeding men to key positions
and galvanizing remaining editors and staff into life. It
was the same one day when an editor, overworked past
endurance, went berserk and attacked him with a foot-long
pair of copy shears. Although he had been a noted boxer
in his young days, the Big Man never made a move
or took his hands out of his pockets while men nearby
restrained his assailant in time.

I call to your attention the phrase "overworked past endurance."

One story—very likely apocryphal—that clung to Hindmarsh throughout his life and into death was that he fired thirteen of his reporters (some accounts make it seven or eight) on Christmas Eve in 1930. Every subsequent Christmas, it was said, the ex-reporters would send their old boss a Merry Christmas telegram, collect.

Morley Callaghan was fired by Hindmarsh four or five times. Each time he simply showed up for work the next day. I've already noted how often he fired his star reporter, Sinclair. But he seemed to take special relish in employing his unique style of management with Ernest Hemingway, whom Hindmarsh considered a prima donna. I wonder if Hindmarsh himself came to realize, before his death, that his only truly lasting legacy would be as Hemingway's tormenter.

Of course, Hemingway wasn't yet Hemingway when he showed up in Hindmarsh's newsroom in September 1923, but he did have a reputation. Morley Callaghan, in his memoir *That Summer in Paris,* remembers being told that the new reporter, whom he hadn't yet met, was a "good newspaperman" who was coming to Toronto from Paris to become the paper's new star. So, on Hemingway's first day on the job, Callaghan was very interested to see which story "the big correspondent from Europe" would be assigned. Checking the assignment ledger Hindmarsh had drawn up, Callaghan was staggered to see Hemingway had been given five crummy cub assignments, the same kind of stuff young Callaghan would be asked to cover. "Our Mr. Hindmarsh was determined that no one should get the impression that he was going to be coddled," he wrote. This was the Hindmarsh treatment.

We don't know what all those five assignments were. According to William Burrill, one of them was a "long, rather dry political piece headlined 'Offer Sir Donald Soviet Railroads.'" We also know, again thanks to Burrill, that

Hemingway was on a train heading east that same night to cover the escape of Norman "Red" Ryan and four other convicts from Kingston Penitentiary.

These early pieces Hemingway wrote for the *Star* were unknown until Burrill identified them. None of them were bylined. Bylines were handed out much less often back then, particularly in Hindmarsh's newsroom, particularly to reporters the boss felt needed to have their egos readjusted. But Burrill tracked down Hemingway's notes, even his train ticket to Kingston, giving us all the opportunity to appreciate writing like this, which is from the first of the four long pieces he filed on the prison break:

> It was so dark that the scout could not see his horse's head. But he heard the fence wires on the south side of the road creak. He shouted to the guards who were further down the road and then there was silence. The four men had their rifles ready.
>
> Then in the dark there was a rush across the road. The guards fired into the dark at the sound and rushed forward. In the dark a man's voice said, "Are you hurt, shorty?" The guards shot again where the voice came from and one of them fired point blank as a man dashed by him toward the north side of the road. The men had crossed

from the south tract of the woods to
the northern half of the seven hundred acres. About fifteen rifle shots
were fired in the dark. There was no
blood and there are no bodies.

Notice the repeated use of the word "dark," what Burrill describes as a "[Gertrude] Stein–like echo effect." Notice also how direct and compact the sentences are. And the words. You don't encounter a word longer than one syllable until the third sentence, other than the possessive of "horse." This is not standard 1920s newspaper writing. This is not a reporter transcribing the quotes he wrote down after interviewing a couple of prison guards. This is the work of a real writer. Oh, and check out that beautiful tense-flip in the last line.

But if Hemingway returned from Kingston expecting praise, or even an upgrading of his assignments, he was mistaken. Hindmarsh kept piling on the menial, cub reporter assignments, working him hard, days, evenings and weekends. By the middle of his first week on the job, according to Burrill, Hemingway was showing signs of exhaustion. But still the weekend assignments and out-of-town trips continued. He was unable to spend much time with his wife, Hadley, who was expecting a child. And in fact, the baby was born while Ernest was on a four-day trip to New York City, where he filed ten stories, working nineteen-hour days. He resented missing the birth very much. He also resented being bawled out by Hindmarsh when he returned to Toronto for not stopping by the office before he visited the hospital.

Now, none of this is to suggest that Ernest Hemingway *wasn't* a prima donna. He very clearly was. But still . . .

J.H. Cranston, who edited the *Star Weekly* at the time, described H.C.H. to Hemingway biographer Charles Fenton as a sadist who "took delight in breaking or humbling men's spirits." He also called him "ambitious, cruel and jealous of the success of others." This is from a colleague. Yet another Hemingway biographer, Michael Reynolds, had this to say about the relationship between the two men: "Within a month they were enemies, and within three months Ernest, without telling Hindmarsh, booked return passage to France."

Ernest Hemingway's leave-taking from the *Star* has become legendary, despite the fact that nobody can seem to agree on the details. Some say his boiling point was reached when Hindmarsh threw out a set of important documents that had been entrusted to Hemingway by a source on the condition that Hemingway would return them. Some (including Gordon Sinclair) say it came when Hindmarsh assigned Hemingway to welcome a white peacock the *Star* had donated to the Toronto Zoo and to launch a contest for readers to name the bird. Being asked to do promotional work was more than he could take.

Whatever the motivation, all the storytellers agree that an enraged Hemingway sat down at his desk and began to type and type . . . and type . . . page after page of bile and vitriol, which he then pasted together into a long sheet and pinned to the office bulletin board. Greenaway said the resignation letter hung down five feet, almost to the floor. Others have it as long as fifteen feet, down to the floor and then curled up in a roll.

However long it was, for three days Hindmarsh ignored it. He walked past it countless times a day, without saying a word, without acknowledging it in any way, until finally someone, maybe Hemingway, maybe not, took it down.

Hemingway hung around until December 26, long enough to get his Christmas bonus, and then was gone. Back to Paris.

According to Callaghan, if it weren't for Hindmarsh, Hemingway would have stuck around Toronto for another year or two and maybe wouldn't have written *The Sun Also Rises*. He called his old boss "the grand antagonist." Clearly, Hemingway hated the man. And it was a grudge that he carried with him for the rest of his life. Or didn't. Accounts vary.

In his memoirs, Roy Greenaway writes that Hemingway eventually buried the hatchet. He has the writer sending a warm, congratulatory telegram to his former boss on the occasion of a banquet in Hindmarsh's honour held about a year before his death.

But Tom Williams, a former reporter for the rival *Evening Telegram*, shared a different remembrance of Hemingway and Hindmarsh in a letter he wrote to the *L.A. Times* in 1992. When Hindmarsh died in 1956, Williams was assigned the job of helping to write the *Tely*'s obituary, and so he called up Hemingway in Havana. After he broke the news,

```
There  was  a  long  silence  and  heavy
breathing.  "Mr.  Williams,"  said  Heming-
way,  "this  started  out  as  a  shitty
day.  It  is  raining  and  cold  and  my
old  wounds  are  bothering  me.  I  ran
```

```
into bad rum last night." Pause
and more breathing. "He is really
dead, you say?" I assured him. More
chuckles and then hellish laugh-
ter. "That saves me killing him,"
said Hemingway. Finally, we managed
to agree on a publishable quote—
something like—"Mr. Hindmarsh was a
rare figure in Canadian journalism
and we will not see his like again."
To which Hemingway probably added:
"Thank God!"
```

It will no doubt surprise you to learn that Harry Hindmarsh was also a cartoon character. Yes, indeed. He appears in a National Film Board of Canada cartoon series called *The Dark Years*, all about the Great Depression. Red Ryan is in it too. And Gordon Sinclair. The whole gang. In fact, Hindmarsh does more than just appear. He narrates the three-part series, which was made in 2008 and combines different types of animation with archival footage and old still photography, live actors and interviews with people who lived through the Depression, including our very own Jocko Thomas.

Episode 2 is the one that features Ryan. It begins with a smiling H.C.H. sitting behind a big desk in his office at the Toronto Star Building. He's wearing a white shirt with a black vest and a blue tie, loose at the neck. He's drawn as a round-faced, balding man, wearing round, steel-framed glasses. He actually looks quite jolly.

Most of the episode deals with the battles fought by Prime Minister R.B. Bennett against the communists, the Canadian Labour Defence League and the Relief Camp Workers Union, culminating in the On to Ottawa trek and the Market Square riot in Regina. Mixed in are assorted Depression horror stories and the birth of the Dionne quintuplets. That's where an animated Gordon Sinclair makes his appearance.

The Red Ryan section comes near the end of the episode. It's set up with a montage of wanted posters from the United States, featuring all the A-list crooks: John Dillinger, Pretty Boy Floyd, Ma Barker, Bonnie and Clyde, and lastly Canada's own Red Ryan. Hindmarsh narrates: "Bank robbers became folk heroes to many working people in the 1930s, and newspapers had a lot to do with it."

We see the highlights of Ryan's career: the escape in the smoke at Kingston, our man vaulting bank counters during his robberies, his capture in Minneapolis and finally Ryan, alone, in solitary. That's when we first hear him speak, in voice-over, sounding very *Guys and Dolls*-y: "As I always had a Bible beside me in my cell, I took to reading it to pass the time away. I have no doubt its splendid passages helped crystalize my purpose to reform."

I should point out that the cartoon Red Ryan looks nothing like the non-cartoon version. He's drawn blocky and squat, with bright orange hair over a broken-nosed face. His eyes, pale blue and small in real life, are large and jet black, the artists clearly going for a windows-on-the-soul effect.

But these filmmakers have done their research. His jailhouse chat with the prime minister is word-for-word accurate. Narrator Hindmarsh tells us, "When Mr. Ryan was released a year later, the prime minister, for once, had our paper's support." And the real Jocko Thomas adds, "Red Ryan became a darling of the *Star*, and the *Star* champeened, more or less, the release of Red Ryan." He actually says "champeened," like he's a corner man for Stanley Ketchel.

Ryan's time in the spotlight and return to crime are also very accurately portrayed. The botched Sarnia robbery is more true to life than most of the accounts of it written by journalists. As Ryan lies bleeding out at the bottom of the liquor store stairs, the film cuts to his body lying under a sheet on a slab at the morgue. His eyes are open, staring lifelessly, and for the first time they are not pure black. They are pale brown, ringed with red. Still not accurate, but very effective.

Jocko Thomas tells us, "The *Star* had egg all over its face

after that, because here we were champeening Red Ryan. . . .
But it sold a lot of papers."

It absolutely did.

ALL GOOD REPORTERS are competitive. They live to beat the
other guys, both competitors and colleagues. But it's generally
an ego thing. It's about reputation and bragging rights. Very
few journalists are competitive for reasons of the bottom line.
Hindmarsh was a bottom-line guy. He wanted the story first
because he wanted the *Star* to continue to make more money
than the *Globe* and the *Tely*. It was his father-in-law's paper,
after all, and it was coming to him. He could make more
money by driving his reporters harder than the reporters were
driven at the other papers, so that he would get the stories the
readers wanted before the other papers.

And he knew very well what the readers wanted. The public
wanted to be entertained, and crime was entertainment. The
famous crooks all had nicknames, just like ballplayers. Baby
Face Nelson. Pretty Boy Floyd. And, of course, the Golden
Boy of Crime, Red Ryan. If the public wanted to read about
famous bank robbers, the *Star* would give them one. The best
bank robber of them all. The Ace.

Consequences never entered into any of this. Even years
later, in his memoirs, Greenaway writes about the Ryan story
as if it were a great success, a wild journalistic romp. He begins
his chapter on Ryan with the line "The 'Red' Ryan story was
mine." He doesn't start with "Let me tell you how I helped

kill a cop." Later in the chapter, writing about the night he arranged to sneak Ryan off his train to Toronto so the *Star* would have the story all to itself, he writes, "The Toronto morning papers were puzzled as to why Ryan had not arrived at Union Station. Meanwhile I went to the *Star*'s editorial room and wrote all night. It was a major scoop." It would also be a major scoop the following year when Ryan was connected to the shooting death of Edward Stonehouse.

But that's all they were. Scoops. No one, least of all Greenaway, considered publicly whether a connection existed between them. Greenaway can write movingly about the great anguish experienced by Father Kingsley, the man who was betrayed by his acolyte, Red Ryan. But he is incapable of writing about the Lewis and Stonehouse blood on the hands of the little priest with the big ego, because then he'd be forced to look at his own hands, and the hands of Harry Hindmarsh. They were just stories. All that mattered was getting them first.

When Harry Hindmarsh died, he was eulogized for his immense contributions to the newspaper industry and praised for the causes championed by the *Star* under his leadership, things like unemployment insurance and the baby bonus. He and his paper were said to have had an enormous and positive effect on the lives of Canadians.

Maybe that's true. Maybe he was a great man. But I suspect he viewed social causes the same way he viewed bank robbers, as a way to make his competition look bad, and sell more papers.

And if all those positive benefits were just accidental by-products of Hindmarsh's drive to beat his competitors, how much credit should he get? And if we do credit him for all the great changes in society the *Star* helped usher in, then how much blame does he shoulder for the death of Constable John Lewis?

Saturday Book Review
William Arthur Deacon Literary Editor

Life and Death of Red Ryan

MORE JOY IN HEAVEN. By Morley Callaghan. Macmillan, $2.75

News values predominate in Morley Callaghan's new novel. So closely is this story patterned on the final phases of the career of the Toronto bank robber, Red Ryan, that local readers will hardly regard it as fiction, and must lose sight of artistic values. Despite use of the name Delaware, we find Sherbourne Street mentioned, and Queen's Park, Maple Leaf Gardens and other spots unmistakably described.

Morley Callaghan

The main trend of the tale is the miraculous reform in prison of a man of violence, the sympathy of a clergyman, the powerful interest of a highly placed politician, the jailbird's release, the life of Riley that he led, for a time and which culminated in his death at a robbery. Of course details are changed here and there, but parallels or identities abound. For example, we all remember the pathetic question of the young nephew about the death of Uncle Norman, who had become a hero to the boy. In the book this becomes: "Oh, gee, the kids say my Uncle Kip shot a cop; Why would Uncle Kip shoot a cop?" In the same connection we have the respectable brother who changed his name so as to escape contamination from the criminal's repute.

As novelist Mr. Callaghan is concerned mainly with psychological explanations of why things went wrong. Being the sort of man he is, Mr. Callaghan is entirely sympathetic with the released man and blames his friends and the public for the tragedy. Yet the author is by no means blind to the uglier realities and suggests pointedly that the disaster was inevitable in the circumstances. Publicity turned a head none too level, anyway, and the case is somewhat like that of a famous college athlete, who may be spoiled for earning his living in ordinary pursuits.

Here, then, is the emotional Kip Caley, who has reformed at Kingston and is let out. The papers play him up, which he finally permits to get some cash to help the family of a crook. The only job provided is that of host in a hotel with night club attached. So long as Kip is notorious he gets good pay and is free to advise and befriend less fortunate released men. But the public is fickle and soon loses interest in unspectacular virtue. Having feasted the prodigal son, it is ready to forget him; and while Toronto rejoices over the repentant sinner more than over past persons, the city humanly declines to go on being excited or maintain its worship.

most standardized in its simplicity. Somebody has lately said that Ernest Hemingway heard himself called naive so often that he spent ten years trying to live up to the description. Mr. Callaghan is already in danger of identifying himself so closely with a set type of character, with a single approach to social problems, that his fiction is ceasing to be adventurous and is becoming an easily recognized brand. When that happens his growth will be over. His sales will likely increase, because people like to know in advance precisely what they are buying; but critical interest in his performance will wane as soon as he can be safely ticketed.

I wish time and space permitted a thesis on the word "important" as it is used over and over in "More Joy in Heaven." People feel or are made to feel important. The word becomes a shield for the ego. The criminal's artificially stimulated conceit is not the only case in the story, which is permeated with selfishness of various kinds. The development of some of these would have strengthened the story and given it a variety that it lacks. It might even be guessed that the reiteration of "important" tells things outside the covers altogether. As used in all its connotations, it becomes a mere mannerism.

Mr. Callaghan's career is becoming spiral. Last year's "Now That April's Here" was a collection of short stories similar in content to his original "A Native Argosy," but on a plane immensely higher. His first novel nine years ago, "Strange Fugitive," ended in the death of a gunman in a battle with police; and here we are in "More Joy in Heaven" back in the same surroundings. That Mr. Callaghan has progressed between the two is obvious. Just how far it is impossible for local appraisal to determine since his townsmen must see his latest book mainly as a commentary on the life and death of Red Ryan.

But the new novel does explain the author's recent dictum that there is no difference except length between a novel and a short story. "More Joy in Heaven" is so episodic that it falls within the definition of the expanded short story.

Narrator Prizes

For choosing the best ten books to take to a desert island, and justifying those choices, The Narrator, having received entries from eight Provinces, has awarded prizes as follows: First, R. E. Sneyd, CP.CT, Toronto; special prize, Miss Mary Laird Mark, 419 Brant Street, Woodstock; second, Miss H. M. Yake, Apt. 16, 120 Vaughan Road, Toronto; third, Mrs. B. L. Small, Skead, Ont.; fourth, Miss Marion W. Gray, 202 Humberside Avenue, Toronto; fifth, Miss Ruth Walker, R.R. 3, Metcalfe, Ont.

One Modern Library book, title to be chosen by the winner, has been

Poetry Night:
At Convocati 24, under the the Canadian Poetry Magazine, the autho figure: Top, left, his Excellency Lord Twee Sir Charles G. D. Roberts. Second row, fro MacDonald, E. J. Pratt (editor), Pelham man), the late T. B. Roberton (medallist) from left, Bertram Brooker (medallist), G Clarke (Seranus Prize), Nathaniel A. Katherine Hale.

muir's speech, five-minute readings by six poets—Roberts, Pratt, MacDonald, Hale, Clarke and Benso— and the initial presentation of The Governor-General's Annual Literary Awards, arranged by the Canadian Authors' Association for Fiction and General Literature. It is sad that Mrs. M. M. Howard, donor of the Seranus Prize for poetry, died just before its first presentation : :

Pherson, and are on the realized what cellor. He p of a hundred child plays w not know wh the amount o into a demon ronto Book P tives, speaker with special

CHAPTER 17

MORE JOY

17

I don't think you can put yourself in other people's positions.
Nor should you. All you can do is occupy your own,
as fully as possible . . .
—Emmanuel Carrère, in the *Paris Review*

L et me tell you about my central failure in this book. There
are many, but this one is key. Since I started working on
this jumbled ramble I have tried without success to imagine
what it must be like to be Red Ryan, how it would feel to wake
up in the morning inside his head. I have circled and circled,
but never really gotten close to penetrating the hard surface of
the man.

I can't imagine, for example, what would propel a man
to rob a bank, unless it were an act of pure desperation, the
need to feed a starving child, say. But as an act of public declaration? An assertion of identity? I can't fathom that kind of
thinking.

I can certainly appreciate the exhilaration one would feel after a successful bank robbery. (Unless someone was hurt, of course. Or killed.) I can imagine the surging euphoria—I smile at the thought of it—as you stare at your stacks of money, knowing that you've done it. You've actually gotten away with it. The police will not be knocking on your door. Anyone who has ever gotten away with anything can magnify that sensation and put themselves in that room. But that enormous relief, that feeling of dodging the literal bullet would only ensure, in my case, that I would never be so foolish as to tempt fate in such an enormous way again.

For Ryan, though, the thrill seemed to come from the act itself, rather than from its successful conclusion. For me, the act of robbing a bank would be the thing that stopped me in my tracks, despite the possibility of stacks of money afterwards. For him, the act of robbing the bank was the attraction; the money was practically beside the point.

This is not to suggest that I'm too good a person to consider stealing. I assure you that is not the case. I'm just as bad as everyone else. But perhaps the key is not whether you are a good person or a bad person. Perhaps it's knowing where—within yourself—goodness and badness can be found.

Perhaps my failure of imagination comes down to an inability to get inside the head of a man who knows *what* goodness and badness are, but doesn't know *where* they are.

Because it can't simply be the same thing as imagining yourself inside the mind of an animal. It isn't simply a flow of basic urges and actions, with no room for or conception of anything as deep as consequences. No, it's more complicated than that. Because in Ryan's head there is language. There is abstract thought. He may not consider consequences. He may not possess morality. But he is aware that such things as consequences and morality exist. He understands these things, in that he would be able to define them if asked; they just don't exist for him in anything other than their dictionary form.

But again, is that right? It can't be possible that concepts like goodness and badness are as irrelevant to him as concepts like karma or feng shui are to me, for the simple reason that I can live my life easily and openly admitting to everyone I meet that I have no time whatsoever for feng shui. I could begin every conversation by saying, "Let me get one thing straight, right off the top. I don't believe in karma."

But Ryan has to pretend, not only that morality matters, but that he possesses it. He has to maintain the illusion that he considers the consequences of his actions, and that he is capable of feelings of guilt and, more profoundly, remorse. So, not only is he aware of what morality means, he is also aware that it is a condition to which he should aspire. This suggests that he is both deeply deficient in the virtues we admire, and profoundly aware of those deficiencies.

Should that knowledge trigger feelings of pity towards Ryan, or should it trigger feelings of fear?

One other thing I've been considering, without much success: What fills the void where the morality should be? What does he feel *instead of* remorse? If it is pure ego, then what kind of tension is set up in the mind of a human being whose every thought, every urge, every desire is accompanied by the knowledge that—whatever it is—it is not only a perfect expression of who he is, it is also wrong? I imagine the answer to that depends on the degree to which this person cares about his deficiencies. Does his self-awareness create feelings of inadequacy? Does he feel he is lacking something fundamentally human? Or is he indifferent to such self-awareness? And is the answer to these questions always the same?

We can look inside ourselves for guidance. We can examine our own justifications and self-recriminations when our egos get the better of our morality, but we can never know how close that takes us to the inner workings of a mind like Ryan's, because we can never know the degree to which he actually cares. We can only empathize as far as the limits of our understanding.

So, how did Morley Callaghan do it? He wrote a novel based on Ryan. How did a writer so uniquely focused on exploring the darkest corners of our motivations and our concepts of right and wrong, good and evil, imagine himself inside the head of a man so profoundly disinterested in those things? Part of the answer to that can be found in the quotation that opens this chapter, because, in the end, Callaghan didn't try to penetrate the mind of Red Ryan. That's not what *More Joy in Heaven* was about.

In Callaghan's novel based on Red Ryan, the hero, Kip Caley, is released from prison at dawn on Christmas Day. It is, he says, "The most beautiful morning in all history."

Like Ryan, Caley is the country's most notorious bank robber. Like Ryan he repents his past thanks to the ministrations of a prison chaplain. A senator helps arrange his early release. A city welcomes him back. He's given work in a hotel

by a wrestling promoter. There is only one significant difference between Kip Caley and Red Ryan: Kip Caley honestly
did undergo a true change of heart during his imprisonment.

It's not by accident that Caley is released early Christmas
morning. Nor is it accidental when, later that day, a reporter
tells him it's his birthday and an ex-con calls him "the light
of the world." If the real-life Ryan was sold to the public as
the prodigal son, who was lost and then, miraculously, found,
the Callaghan version is written as a Messiah figure, as full of
doubts and good intentions as the original.

Outwardly, the plot of the book follows the broad outlines
of the Ryan story. Inwardly, it couldn't be more different. Let
me just pick out a few examples to illustrate what I mean.

When Caley is released from prison, he's dropped off at his
mother's home. He has a long, tender reunion with his mother
and brother. The sound of pounding on the door continues
throughout. It's the press and the neighbours. Finally, Kip's
brother suggests opening the door; otherwise, he says, "they'll
be pounding all night." Kip grabs his brother's arm.

> *"Don't let them in, see?" he begged. "I don't want any-*
> *body to pay attention to me. Tell them to go home. Let*
> *them pound all night. Please, Denis." Then he stopped and*
> *sighed, full of sadness, and he whispered, "Why can't they*
> *leave me alone?"*

When the reporters finally are let in, Kip's first request to them
is, "Look, you guys. Do something for me, will you? Play this
down. Give me a break."

It's not exactly how the original would have played it.

On New Year's Eve, a big party is held in Kip's honour at the hotel where he's been hired to work as a combination greeter/attraction. He's asked to address the crowd, and after begging off, reluctantly agrees. He ends his remarks by saying he hopes they can "always have this good feeling—It's all you can ask—It's the best thing in the world—" When he finishes speaking, he wipes his face with his handkerchief, and wonders why everyone has gone so silent. It was, Callaghan writes, his apotheosis.

Callaghan ends the chapter on that word, which can have two meanings. It is only by reading further that the author's intent is clear. That moment was the high point in Caley's life, but not the moment of his transcendence.

The high point of the real Ryan's life came either in a bank, with a gun in his hand, or holding the floor with a group of friends, bragging about it afterwards. Transcendence was never on the table.

Later in the book, an out-of-work tailor, driven by poverty to steal a diamond ring, shows up at Kip Caley's room. He wants Kip to hide him from the police. Kip, moved that the man has turned to him, agrees, letting the tailor sleep in his room and even washing the blood from the sleeve of the man's coat. Caley spends the night feeling he has been disloyal to everyone. The next day, he drives to the home of the prison chaplain to confess, trying to impress on the priest his belief that the sympathy he showed to the tailor was part of the same sympathy others had shown him.

By this point in the novel, Caley is becoming more and

more uneasy. He questions the motives of everyone around him as well as his own. He argues with a judge who refuses to accept his reformation and with an old prison acquaintance who is convinced Kip is conning the entire city. He considers both men incapable of believing in anything good and pure. He says the judge makes him feel like he'll "always be on the outside looking in."

It all leads to an inescapable conclusion. He's approached to take part in a bank robbery. He refuses. His girlfriend overhears. She tells the priest, who calls the police. Caley, knowing the robbers are being set up and feeling responsible, heads out to warn them. He arrives at the bank in time to see the police open fire on the robbers. Caley tries to stop it. Fails. And in a blind, helpless rage shoots one of the cops dead. He is shot himself and dies, without saying a word, three days later.

There are very few characters in literature more unlike Red Ryan than Kip Caley. Yet their ends are the same. Both men are shot to death after killing a cop.

In this book Callaghan is not only probing the line between sinner and saint, he is asking penetrating questions about our inability to distinguish between the two. If two men, one with goodwill in his heart and the other with larceny, are placed in the same situation and come to the same, terrible end, what are we to take away from that?

But, of course, that's an unfair question. Unfair to Callaghan. *More Joy in Heaven* does not require the Ryan story sitting next to it to make it complete. Because, in the end, this isn't a book about Red Ryan, it's a book about us. It's about society. The great, shifting herd.

We are so quick to embrace, when instructed to embrace, regardless of the facts of the matter. And so quick to turn against, when we have been told our faith has been betrayed.

The goodwill demonstrated by the people of Toronto was betrayed by Red Ryan; the people of Callaghan's Toronto were not betrayed by Kip Caley. But they scream for his blood just the same. The police who had happily patted him on the back at his release donate blood to keep him alive after he's shot, so as not to be cheated of a hanging. The police chief, who had posed with Caley for newspaper pictures, promises to set up the gallows in Caley's hospital room, if necessary.

None of them are able to look any deeper than his final act of violence. If anyone had suggested that perhaps it was Caley who had been betrayed, they would have been shouted down violently. A crowd is no place for shades of grey.

This is who we are.

I'm not going to presume to try to explain Callaghan's intent as an artist, but there is a moment very early in the book when Caley's benefactor, Senator Maclean, performs an act that displays rare self-knowledge. Knowing he himself has a weakness for showing off publicly, for making what he calls "showy gestures to the nation," he asks himself a question as he waits for Caley outside the prison gates: "What's there in it for me?" When he answers that question with "Nothing at all," he is relieved, having determined his motives are pure.

Purity of motive is a knot that Callaghan worked at throughout his career. Caley wrestles with it all through this book. He knows the badness he's capable of, because he's done almost all of it in his life.

We all, secretly, fear the things we believe ourselves capable of doing. What's curious is that this deep truth doesn't move us towards greater empathy, as it seems it logically should; it moves us the other way, towards condemnation, towards blindness and hatred.

In a reminiscence of Callaghan written almost twenty years after his death, the writer Norman Snider said of his friend, "Callaghan understood the nobility of independence. He believed that our whole society was held together by secondhand opinion, and that the man who made his own judgments was an outlaw, even if just in his own living room."

We like to keep things simple. Saints on one side, sinners on the other. Tell us which is which and we'll take care of the rest. Just, please, don't ask us to decide for ourselves. By flipping the true nature of the character at the centre of the Red Ryan story, *More Joy in Heaven* allows us to see what we miss by blindly following the official narrative. And it urges us to ask the messenger, whether it's a politician, a priest, a journalist or a bank robber, What's in it for them?

It's a risky thing, this idea of a society of living-room outlaws, of people capable of standing back and clearly looking at things, of actually seeing for ourselves, and it's probably far beyond our capacity. The risk is in the empathy, in the discovery that not only are our heroes seldom what they seem, but our villains are often much more like us than we admit.

But if we could pull it off, we might come to understand that the only reason we put locks on the playground swing sets is because we so desperately want to swing.

CHAPTER
18

ALONZO

18

I will always cut a lot of slack to the newspaper reporters and editors working in the so-called golden age of print journalism. They had a lot of hungry beasts to feed.

A daily newspaper back then was so much more than the name implies. There were Bulldog Editions, One, Two and Three Star Editions, Home and Sport Editions, Final Editions, Extras. There were a lot of pages to fill, and the competition was fierce. If a big story was on, you had to keep beating the other papers all day long.

But still, do those pressures really excuse the story that appeared on page 10 of the *Globe and Mail* on September 9, 1952? This was the day after Toronto's newest star bank robber, the heir to Red Ryan, escaped from the Don Jail for the second time. His name was Edwin Alonzo Boyd.

The headline reads "Boyd's Exploits Now Top Careers of Ryan, Mickey" (Mickey McDonald was another noted local thug and murderer). The story appears to be an attempt to bring some historical perspective to Boyd's criminal career. Check out the first paragraph:

> Yesterday's events have made the career of Edwin Alonzo Boyd spectacular enough to surpass the activities of two other infamous figures in Canadian crime, Norman (Red) Ryan and Donald (Mickey) McDonald.

I love the definitiveness of this paragraph. I also love the fact that you know immediately there will be nothing in the way of evidence provided to back up that definitiveness. This paragraph makes a few things abundantly clear: (1) This is a story about nothing. (2) The only reason it exists is because an editor wanted a headline with the names Boyd, Ryan and Mickey in it. (3) If you read this piece all the way through, you run the risk of winding up a little more stupid than you were when you started.

My favourite line in the story is from the section in which the reporter tries to show the similarities between the three men. "Each is—or was," he writes, "in the master criminal category." Master criminal. Right up there with Professor James Moriarty. Or Dr. Fu Manchu.

Here's a little tidbit I picked up reading about master criminal Mickey McDonald. After planning a bank robbery with some fellow crooks in 1939, he got so drunk on the day of the heist that he couldn't go. So he sent his younger brother in his place. An accountant at the bank was shot and killed. Mickey's brother was arrested.

Master criminal Red Ryan, as you know, was shot to death while trying to rob a small-town liquor store. When the police counted all the stolen money in Red's pockets and the change that he'd spilled on the floor during his attempted escape, the total was $394.26.

But what about Edwin Alonzo Boyd? Perhaps he truly was a Napoleon of crime.

When I first mentioned to my father that I was writing a book about a Toronto bank robber, his immediate reply was, "Is it Edwin Alonzo Boyd?" It was a natural reaction. Boyd was a very big deal. At least as big a deal as Red Ryan was in his day. And there are still plenty of people around, like my dad, who remember Boyd. There aren't many left from Ryan's days.

Edwin Alonzo Boyd was dashing. He was handsome. The papers loved comparing his looks to Errol Flynn's, even though they really only shared a moustache. Like Ryan, Boyd was a vaulter of bank counters. He was a family man who gave up his job driving a streetcar because it lacked excitement. He found that excitement by forcing bank employees to fill up his bags with money at the point of a gun. The people loved him, maybe because, unlike Red Ryan and Mickey McDonald, he wasn't a killer. Two of his gang members were hung for killing a cop, but as far as the public was concerned, Boyd was more of a gentleman adventurer than a criminal.

He also had a great middle name.

The first time Boyd and some accomplices escaped from the Don Jail, his gang—the Boyd gang, naturally—went on a terrific bank-robbing spree. One of their holdups was the biggest in Toronto history. The police finally caught up with Boyd in bed, with a briefcase full of money and five loaded pistols.

When he escaped from the Don Jail the second time, it triggered the biggest manhunt in Canadian history. It also triggered a flurry of newspaper stories reminding readers about the exploits of Boyd's great predecessor, Red Ryan.

There were three Ryan pieces written by the long-time columnist for the *Globe and Mail* J.V. McAree. The first, headlined, for some reason unclear to me, "Norman, the Red Ryan," begins:

> It was inevitable that the excitement over the exploits of the Boyd gang should turn the thoughts of many readers to the case of the infamous criminal, Norman (Red) Ryan, which we have been asked to review. Personally we knew little or nothing of Ryan in the days when he was in the newspaper headlines. We had an opportunity to meet him socially on one occasion, but did not take advantage of it.

McAree doesn't mention whether he (they?) regretted missing out on the opportunity to meet the Golden Boy. He moves straight on to a fairly accurate recap of Ryan's life and career. The only glaring error is that McAree has Ryan escaping from Kingston "shielded by a heavy fog," rather than by the smoke the prisoners created by lighting some hay on fire.

But the best thing about this first McAree piece is the reaction it triggered. A little over a month later, McAree wrote a follow-up headlined "Red Ryan Defended." He had received a letter in response to his first column from a Mrs. Margaret Dickenson of Markham, Ontario. Let's just say that Mrs. Dickenson brought a fresh perspective to the final days of our Red.

According to her, Ryan was not involved in the attempted robbery and fatal shooting of Edward Stonehouse in Markham in February 1936. "He was never near Markham at the time of the robbery," she wrote. Nevertheless, the crime had been his undoing: "Ryan went back into the underworld to find the offender, and his deal with the underworld led to the treacherous shooting at Sarnia. The underworld hated him." So Ryan, feigning a return to crime to find the killer of Edward Stonehouse, had been double-crossed by his enemies.

According to Mrs. Dickenson, Ryan never really had a chance to go straight. "He could not remain reformed because the best of those who tried to trust him doubted him in their souls."

McAree passed along one more piece of information from her letter. Mrs. Dickenson said the shooting didn't really kill Edward Stonehouse; it "merely aggravated some disease from which he was suffering." Presumably this disease centred on the area just above his left ear, where Ed McMullen's bullet entered his skull.

I honestly have no idea why McAree wrote the third column about Ryan, which came out about four years after the column featuring Mrs. Dickenson's letter. The headline very simply said, "Red Ryan."

This column is another recap of Ryan's life, this time with no hook to the Boyd gang. In fact there's no real hook at all, except for a brief mention that McAree had been reading a "review" of Ryan's career in *Liberty* magazine. It's as if he forgot he wrote the previous column, which is entirely possible. His career as a columnist began in 1903, so when this edition hit the newsstands, McAree had been writing for the *Globe*'s editorial pages for fifty-three years.

The only part of this column that interests me (aside from McAree's wonderful style) is the tiny sliver of additional light it throws on the meeting between Ryan and McAree that never took place. "We narrowly escaped meeting him," he writes. "If we had, we fear we might, like nearly everybody else, have succumbed to his fatal charm." That's another trait members of the master criminal class tend to have in common: fatal charm.

Ryan, no doubt, would have enjoyed the fact that the antics of Edwin Alonzo Boyd were putting his name back in the papers. What he wouldn't have liked quite so much was that, in a lot of ways, Boyd really was the guy Ryan always claimed to be. Adventurous, but a gentleman. Daring, but not deadly. At least, that's what everyone believed.

Ten days after his second escape from jail, Boyd was

captured without incident in a barn located about a mile up the Don River from the jail. He received eight life sentences and was released from prison after serving fourteen years. Boyd moved to British Columbia, where he lived under an assumed name and drove a bus for disabled people. He married a disabled woman he met on the bus and cared for her and her disabled friend for over twenty-five years in a specially designed home he had built. Edwin Alonzo Boyd died in 2002 at the age of eighty-eight, still the gentleman outlaw.

But just before he died, Boyd made a shocking admission to a journalist named Brian Vallée, who had earlier written a biography of Boyd and made a documentary about the bandit. If true, this admission would permanently alter Boyd's image as a kind of modern-day Robin Hood.

According to Vallée, he was joking to Boyd that he knew more about him than anyone else did when Boyd replied, "You don't know everything about me." Boyd then proceeded to tell Vallée that he was responsible for killing two people. Vallée started doing some research and decided, based on the information Boyd had given him about the circumstances of the killings, that the old bank robber was confessing to an unsolved double murder that had taken place in Toronto in the late 1940s. It was a brutal killing of a man and a woman: he was garrotted; she was strangled to death by the killer's bare hands. Their bodies were dumped in the trunk of a car that was left in High Park. They had simply been in the wrong place at the wrong time.

Boyd died before Vallée was able to set up a filmed confession.

So perhaps Boyd, like his predecessor, was just a malicious little bastard all along. Red Ryan, I think it's safe to say, would have loved hearing that bit of news.

And that's the thing, isn't it? In the end, aren't they all malicious little bastards? Does anyone other than a human being who is broken, either by inclination or circumstance, go into this line of work? Even the original Robin Hood, if there was such a person, hiding out in Sherwood Forest and relieving evil noblemen of their purses, was probably a very unlikeable guy, unless there were ballad writers around.

Still, we loved them, back when gangsters were front-page news. Jesse James and John Dillinger, Bonnie and Clyde. We defended them, just like Mrs. Margaret Dickenson kept on defending poor dead Red. We read about them, and rooted for them. The press knew this—hell, they rooted for them too—so we kept being fed more of them, more of their exploits and daring, more myth and bullshit, until at some point we stopped being interested in gangsters. We found other things to divert us. Today, you hardly ever hear anyone rooting for the bad guy, outside of an election campaign. Is it that the press stopped glorifying them, so we stopped caring? Or did we stop caring, so the press stopped glorifying them?

I think it's more likely the former. As the media became more professional, criminals were treated like criminals. It's pretty tough to argue that today's public fixations show any signs of increased sophistication on our part.

But perhaps it's unfair to exclusively blame the media for our fascination with the darker elements of our world. Maybe it's simply the act of mediation. Just putting a filter or a screen or any sort of distance between us and them seems to do the trick.

Think about the difference between the reaction you have to a photograph of a homeless person (empathy, pity, caring) and your reaction to an actual homeless person on the sidewalk right next to you. That person wrapped in the filthy sleeping bag that you quickly walk around is far too real. Just as running into the actual Eddie Boyd on a dark street in Toronto would be too real.

The stuff in the pictures and in the papers . . . that's just stories.

ACKNOWLEDGEMENTS

T his book has been built chiefly on the long, thorough work of Red Ryan's biographer, Peter McSherry, and on the wild, flowery, fantastic, contradictory, gossip-filled, error-ridden, forgivable and unforgivable work of the newspapermen covering the Red Ryan story in the 1920s and 1930s.

For a greater sense of the man and his times, I can recommend the following books that I've found both crucial in my writing and more than enjoyable on their own merits: Peter McSherry, *The Big Red Fox* (Toronto: Dundurn Press, 1999); Martin Robin, *The Saga of Red Ryan and Other Tales of Violence from Canada's Past* (Saskatoon: Western Producer Prairie Books, 1982); Frank Rasky, *Gay Canadian Rogues* (Winnipeg: Harlequin, 1958); Morley Callaghan, *More Joy in Heaven* (Toronto: McClelland & Stewart, 1960; first published 1937); Morley Callaghan, *That Summer in Paris* (Toronto: Exile Editions, 2015; first published 1963); William Burrill, *Hemingway: The Toronto Years* (Toronto: Doubleday Canada Limited, 1994); Jocko Thomas, *From Police Headquarters*

(Toronto: Stoddart Publishing Co. Limited, 1990); John Boyko, *Bennett: The Rebel Who Challenged and Changed a Nation* (Toronto: Key Porter Books, 2010); and (if you can find a copy) Norman J. Ryan, *"Red" Ryan's Rhymes and Episodes* (Hamilton, ON: Dodge Publishers, 1924).

Most of the derogatory quotes about Toronto I poached from Allan Levine's very entertaining *Toronto: Biography of a City* (Madeira Park, BC: Douglas & McIntyre, 2014). And, while it has nothing to do with either Ryan or his times, for good writing about writing, check out Geoff Dyer's *Out of Sheer Rage* (London: Little, Brown and Company, 1997), from which, speaking of poaching, I lifted an entire sentence. (It's the one that immediately follows my threat of plagiarism.)

Brad Wilson at HarperCollins Canada came up with the idea for this project. To Brad goes my deep thanks for his patience and advice. Thanks also to copy editor Sarah Wight, who did such a tremendous job with this discursive (her word) manuscript, Tara Tovell, Stephanie Conklin and Zeena Baybayan.

My friend Tom Jokinen read the first draft and made many excellent suggestions.

Sharon Cavanagh was my first and last reader, and her input was indispensable.

ILLUSTRATION CREDITS

AP Photo/CP Images: 148

Jim Brown: 121

Canada's Penitentiary Museum: 42, 79, 160, 206

City of Toronto Archives: 13 (Fonds 1257, Series 1057, Item 4188), 79 (Fonds 1266, Item 148347), 109 (Fonds 1231, Item 469), 112 (Fonds 1257, Series 1057, Item 42), 174 (Fonds 1266, Item 5170), 191 (Fonds 1244, Item 1003)

The Globe and Mail: 122, 192, 212, 242

Hulton Archive Collection/Getty Images: 24

Library and Archives Canada: xii, 9 (former accession number RG73-C-6), 105 (Alexandra Studio/PA-052380)

Library of Congress: 31 (New York World-Telegram and the Sun Newspaper Photograph Collection/LC-USZ62-138825)

National Film Board of Canada: 237 (*The Dark Years: Canada During the Great Depression* © 2004 National Film Board of Canada. All rights reserved.)

Toronto Star Archives: 16, 36, 71 (bottom), 72, 86, 130, 141, 145, 156, 173, 222, 227

Toronto Star Archives/Getty Images: 254

Toronto Telegram: 170–71